I0570069

Not My Money

Overcoming the Elephant in the Room

CJ Corki

CJ Corki Publishing LLC
Cleveland, OH

Copyright © 2024 by **CJ Corki**

All rights reserved. No part of this publication may be reproduced, distributed, or transmitted in any form or by any means, without prior written permission.

CJ Corki/CJ Corki Publishing
132a Veterans Lane Suite #342
Doylestown, PA/18901
author@cjcorki.com

Publisher's Note: This is a work of fiction. Names, characters, places, and incidents are a product of the author's imagination or personal experiences. Locales and public names are sometimes used for atmospheric purposes. Any resemblance to actual people, living or dead, or to businesses, companies, events, institutions, or locales is completely coincidental.

Neither the author nor the publisher assumes any responsibility or liability on behalf of the consumer or reader of this material. Any perceived slight of any individual or organization is purely unintentional.

Book Cover Design 2024 - 100 Covers
Font: Open Dyslexic
Not My Money/ CJ Corki-- 1st ed.

ISBN Hardcover: 979-8-9885588-59
ISBN Paperback: 979-8-9885588-42

Dedication

This book is dedicated to our extraordinary parents, Carl and Generose Szostak, the ringmasters of our family circus. Their remarkable skills as both parents and grandparents have kept the show running smoothly. With their wisdom as our guiding trapeze and their support as our safety net, they have orchestrated a spectacular performance. We applaud their tireless dedication and hard work, making our family the greatest show on earth.

TABLE OF CONTENTS

Introduction

Join us under the big top as we explore the six different elephants in the room: Financial, Intellectual, Human, Social, Spiritual, and Legacy Capitals. Each pachyderm holds the power to transform the rising generation's lives and shape their future. Financial Capital refers to assets and wealth, Intellectual Capital involves knowledge and innovation, Human Capital focuses on skills and education, Social Capital highlights relationships and family bonds, Spiritual Capital emphasizes values and beliefs, and Legacy Capital encompasses the impact you have on future generations.

Let's step into the circus tent to witness inspiring performances. These performances feature stories that vividly illustrate the transformative power and significance of each type of capital. After the show, you will have the chance to join the joyful parade of elephants, marching in a line with their trunks held high, celebrating the enriched life you have created. Let the show begin!

Chapter 1

Financial Capital: Preparing Grandkids for Financial Success

"Money is a life skill – and as parents, grandparents, interested adults – it's up to us to make sure our children are prepared for the financial world they are going to face."

Sharon Lechter

Financial Capital Introduction

Capital is often associated with money but can also take the form of assets such as cash, public securities, private company stocks, and interests in private partnerships. For grandparents, Financial Capital can include savings, investments, property, and other valuable assets. Teaching kids about financial management means helping them understand how to use, save, and achieve financial goals. These essential skills should be part of a family's plan to create independent, well-informed adults. We hope to demonstrate how you can make a difference in your grandchildren's lives by encouraging you to teach them the various forms of Capital. At the conclusion of each chapter, there will be a guide to help you track and implement your ideas. Let's begin with Financial.

Money Matters for Kids: Teaching Financial Capital

As grandparents, we cherish the moments we spend with our grandchildren. It's a time to impart wisdom, share stories, and teach essential life lessons. Among these, one of the most valuable lessons we can pass on is about Financial Capital – the money stuff that shapes their future. In this chapter, we'll explore why teaching kids about money is vital from a grandparent's perspective and offer practical tips for helping them understand its significance.

For us grandparents, seeing our grandchildren grow and learn is a joy. But why start teaching them about Financial Capital early? Kids are like sponges, eager to absorb knowledge. By teaching them about money early on, we lay the foundation for a lifetime of responsible financial habits.

Grandparents have a wealth of life experiences from which to draw. We can share stories of our financial triumphs and mistakes, offering invaluable insights to our grandkids. These stories make financial lessons relatable and memorable.

As a loving grandparent, imparting valuable lessons about money to your grandchildren is important. First and foremost, share the concept that money is earned through hard work and providing services, drawing from your own life experiences to emphasize the virtues of dedication. Teach them the importance of saving, introduce the notion of a piggy bank or savings account, and illustrate the joy of achieving savings goals, whether for a special toy or their future college education. Next, instill the wisdom of spending wisely, helping them discern needs and wants, and involving them in family spending decisions to demonstrate how money is allocated for essentials and savings. As they grow, introduce them to budgeting, assisting them in creating a simple budget to allocate funds for saving, spending, and giving to charity. Moreover, it explains how money saved in a bank account can accrue interest over time and, for older grandchildren, introduces the basics of investing, highlighting the importance of long-term financial planning. Finally, they share the benefits of patience and delayed gratification, revealing that waiting for something they desire can yield far greater rewards than impulsive, instant purchases. These invaluable lessons will help guide your grandchildren toward a secure and prosperous financial future.

There are numerous engaging and educational activities to share with your grandchildren that can instill valuable financial lessons. Monopoly, the timeless board game, offers a fun way to teach buying, selling, and property management, all while providing an excellent opportunity for quality time together. You can also create a simple allowance tracker to help them grasp the concepts of earning, saving, and spending money, fostering financial responsibility from an early age. Taking them grocery shopping and involving them in price comparisons and budgeting provides a real-life lesson that will leave a lasting impression. Additionally, sharing age-appropriate financial books that explain key concepts in a relatable and enjoyable manner promotes financial literacy and creates a meaningful bonding experience as you read together. These activities contribute to a well-rounded financial education for your grandchildren.

Help your grandchildren set financial goals, whether it's saving for a special toy, a future adventure, or a charity they want to support. Please encourage them to create a visual representation of their goals, such as a collage or vision board.

As grandparents, we have a unique opportunity to lead by example. Involve your grandchildren in financial discussions, showing them how you save, budget, and make informed financial decisions. Your actions speak louder than words.

Take your grandkids to the bank to open a savings account or let them pay for small purchases to help them understand the value of money. Please encourage them to participate in charitable activities to teach them the importance of giving back.

Teaching your grandchildren about Financial Capital is a priceless gift that will guide them toward economic success and security. As a grandparent, you create a legacy that will benefit your grandchildren and future generations. The lessons they learn today will empower them to make informed financial decisions, achieve their money goals, and secure their financial future. Start early, share your wisdom, and watch your grandchildren flourish as financially savvy individuals, all thanks to your guidance and love.

Creating a Family Economy: Ditching the Kid's Allowances, Maybe

Setting up a family economy is a fun way to teach children about Financial Capital and the value of money. Give it a try!

Growing up, I never received an allowance. The expectation on Saturday morning was to work through the list of choirs my mom left for us before she went to work. Doing the dishes, sweeping the floor, dusting the furniture, and vacuuming the rug were all part of the Saturday list. My mom raised five daughters while working full time, so having everyone chip in was essential to maintaining the house. Yes, my dad chipped in too. He oversaw maintenance, cutting the grass, fixing appliances, and plowing the snow. We observed our parents working two or more jobs to pay for parochial schools and our college education. We knew early in life that there was no such thing as a "Free Lunch."

Fast-forward to college. My Economics professor explained the principles of supply and demand. He clearly stated that there are no easy shortcuts to success in life, "No Free Lunch." But waiting to learn that lesson in college seems a little late. My family established a family economy because we didn't have much. It was out of necessity. Shouldn't every family teach finance basics before their kids are off alone?

So, what is a "Family Economy?" It is learning about earning, saving, spending, and giving money with the safety of making mistakes within the family unit and making it clear that money is something you must EARN. With that definition, why would you give an allowance? Isn't that free money? Maybe.

Although I never had an allowance, I worked in the family business since I could walk. It might have only been ten cents an hour, but I learned to count very early with money. I always had money as a child and could spend it on whatever I wanted. My parents supplied the basic needs of food, clothing, and shelter, but my hobbies were mine to purchase. My sister would buy knitting items, but I would buy figurines to paint. Although I was granted this freedom, the first and foremost lesson was to save money for college. Yes, at six years of age, I was saving for the future and learning the time value of money.

However, a typical child in today's society would not be able to get a job before turning 16. So, how do you prepare them to be financially literate? Yes, it might be wise to introduce an allowance, but with lessons about responsibilities. You need to support the expectation of a chore list to earn an allowance to learn lessons on finance. But work with your children on ways to earn additional money. List how they could make more money by doing things above their everyday work. Wash the car? Weed the garden? Anything not in their everyday expectation would work. And let them pick and choose what they would like to do. Get their input on ideas. Maybe a lemonade stands or shoveling the neighbor's driveway?

Once they understand how to earn money, save, spend, and give, go on the list of lessons to learn. As a grandparent, don't waste the opportunity for financial lessons by spoiling your grandchildren with "Free Lunches." Use the opportunity to facilitate financial acumen by assisting your grandchildren in learning about how they could earn.

My parents had a white picket fence that needed constant repair and painting. Our children learned early on how to do the hard work of painting a wall. No, it isn't fun. No, it isn't exciting work. But it was work, and my kids earned five dollars for a well-done job—excellent lessons on earning.

What can you teach your grandchildren about earning money? Are there chores you can give them to earn extra cash? How can you facilitate the lesson of "No Free Lunch?" As a grandparent, your wisdom of earning, saving, spending, and giving can make a difference.

Getting Your Hand Stuck In the Cookie Jar and Other Financial Lessons

Fiscal responsibility is something that needs to be taught at an early age. Parents should intentionally educate their children to be money-aware. It will not be a lesson in their school nor an example set by our government. Parents need to demonstrate that money does not grow on trees by talking about earning cash through allowances and, eventually, jobs. I started working in our family business as soon as I could walk. I would get ten cents for restocking the candy display. Eventually, I worked up to organizing and ordering the merchandise. However, the big honor was creating fantastic Easter baskets, considering the cost of what was inside for reasonable pricing. Business families, unfortunately, get into the rut of children thinking that life is like a cookie jar they can reach into any time they need money. It starts with a cookie but evolves into high expectations of having everything paid for them.

Do your kids expect a car for their sixteenth birthday?

I did not get a car for my birthday when I was sixteen. Our children did not get one either. However, this seems to be the norm today. We did give our boys a used car they could share. This decision taught them how to work together and prioritize vehicle use. Did they need the car to go to work or soccer practice? That would take priority over going to a friend's house to hang out or other non-essential activities. If your child wants a car, the lesson of obtaining a loan, paying for insurance, or, at the very least, paying for gas is a learning opportunity. For many families, this is a missed chance to teach the value of money, but it should start earlier than the teenage years.

My mom taught me math in first grade by giving me change in a cash register drawer. I used that example with our children with an old-fashioned register. When our son was three years old, he could count the coins he put into plastic baggies, each equal to a dollar. We would then go to the educational store to allow him to buy his items. Note that I said an educational store, not a toy store. We encourage our boys to play games to help with their development instead of the famous Ninja turtle figures.

We expanded their money expertise with games like Monopoly and Cash Flow as they grew. They learned the consequences of their decisions based on the choices made. Cash Flow had a budget component that I thought was valuable but backfired on me as a parent. I did not want them to have an X-box to play video games mindlessly. The boys had a different idea. Working together, they put a budget together on how they planned to purchase the game if I gave my permission. Their ingenuity needed to be rewarded, and I accepted their plan for a purchase.

Then there is the cookie-jar kid mentality. "Mom, can I have a cookie?" they would ask. It sounds like a simple request until it expands to "I need that new expensive dress for prom" or "Can you fly me to New York to see my boyfriend?" And eventually, as an adult, "Mom, Dad, I cannot find a job. Will you pay for my living expenses?"

I cannot comment on this since our boys have been fiscally responsible. However, they had experienced friends from a very wealthy neighborhood who fell into this category. Our middle son once said, "If you give your kid everything, they expect everything from everyone." This profound statement initiated our withdrawal of our boys from the exclusive private school they attended. Even though we valued the highest education possible for our children, the influence of their peers was not worth the risk.

Having a family development plan is critical to the next generation's success. 70% of wealth transfers will fail in the next generation. If that does not give you a reason to look into succession planning, what will? Stop the cookie jar mentality and educate the next generation about money and responsibility.

What are you doing with your family to educate them on finances? Do they know their coins and dollar bills?

Quarter Time: Teaching the Next Gen about Finance

Start by teaching them about pennies, nickels, dimes, and quarters. Growing up, my parents taught their five daughters a lot about money. Bills and coins surrounded us since we worked in a family business. My aunt would iron the crinkly bills to keep things in order and not even think about having them face in different directions, a big no-no. We would neatly and accurately count the piles of bills, sorting them by ones, fives, tens, and twenties. Honesty and Integrity were a given. Although pocketing a few loose bills might be tempting, we never did.

Besides honesty, they also taught us about paying it forward. My dad always brought coins when visiting my aunt's house. Their kids would be given a shiny new quarter when we arrived. My dad would direct my cousins to save this money for college. It was our family's mantra to "Save for College." I remember hearing it repeatedly. Since my parents didn't have an opportunity to receive a college degree, they stressed the importance of saving for the event. My happy cousins were gleeful about receiving the gift; my dad was just as pleased about giving it, especially to the next generation.

"Keep the change," we were told when my parents would ask us to purchase an item. They would give us $5 for an item costing $3.50. They would ask us to keep the change when returning the money. Of course, with the expectation of saving it for college. But we learned that those little additions of cash would add up. We never got an allowance, so keeping the change was a solution to learning about saving.

"Find a penny, pick it up; you will have good luck all day." Most people today don't exert the energy to pick up a lonely penny. I am compelled to do so still. First of all, I was taught to be a coin collector. What if that penny is old and worth more than a penny? I always look for the date first. The second reason is the penny's symbolism; It represents new beginnings, a new chapter, and a fresh start. Third, finding a penny is a sign that wealth is coming. But the most important reason I pick up a penny is that I believe the penny is a sign that our guardian angel is watching over us—a message from heaven.

However, my parent's lesson was that even a penny could accumulate to significance. Like the riddle, "Would you rather have a penny today that doubled every day for a month or $1 million today?" If you haven't taught your children or grandchildren yet about the time value of money, put it on your to-do list. An easy way to explain it to young children is to reference a chart. The critical takeaway is to save early and often.

Working in a family business also taught me math by counting. My mom would have me count changes from a cash register drawer in first grade. Although I couldn't see over the counter, my accuracy was perfect, down to the penny. Playing pretend store with grandkids is a fun activity. You can buy a cash drawer anywhere, and by using real money, they will feel grown up.

For young children, start with quarters to teach them how much a dollar is worth. At two years old, my son learned to put four quarters in a baggie to add up to a dollar. We would then go to the educational store to see what could be purchased. Once they understand the quarter, you can graduate to other coins. Using our placemat to count with coins is another fun learning tool.

The importance of teaching grandkids about money early cannot be stressed enough. They should learn how to earn, count, save, and give it away to charity. Many parents aren't comfortable talking to their children about money, so ensure they are on board with the life lessons you share with their kids. Show them the number of core values that could be learned, including honesty, integrity, wealth, debt, generosity, personal responsibility, and stewardship. Look for fun activities to demonstrate how to raise financially responsible children, including being a role model.

Sixteen Cents Minus 7 Cents = What?

Can your grandchildren count change? It is crucial to impart basic mathematical skills to young individuals so they do not have to rely solely on technological devices like computers, cash registers, or calculators. Starting early with teaching them how to count money can help them become more self-sufficient when entering the workforce.

My sisters and I learned how to make change even before we were tall enough to reach the cash register at our family's store. We remember our great aunt counting the money the store took that day. We would be watching the Wonderful World Of Color while she sat at the table. She would count the cash, then count it again. If it didn't match, she would grumble and count it again, this time in aggravated Polish. We learned to count in Polish this way, though we were more interested in watching TV.

Today, we are all accustomed to pulling out our plastic credit cards. Unfortunately, our grandchildren don't enjoy the tactile and mental challenge of handling cash.

Here are some simple and fun games you can play with your grandkids to help them with math and learning how to count money:

From simple to harder:
1). Place a bunch of money (including change) on the table and have the child organize them by denomination. Teach them to stack the bills with the fronts all facing up and each bill facing in the same direction (We learned this from our Great Aunt). This is common for bank tellers and retail shop owners who must take the cash to the bank.

2). Ask the child to give you exactly $7.36 from this stack. Do this numerous times with different amounts. To make it more fun, have your grandchild ask you to provide them with exact money. You can do several rounds of back-and-forth.

3). A corollary to this is to ask them to give you $0.42 and then ask how many ways they can make money equal to $0.42: a quarter/nickel/dime and two pennies, four dimes, two pennies, etc.

4). Now for the challenge rounds: Tell the child something costs $6.42. You give them $20. This change game is vital since it teaches the child to do math in their head.

5). Now, you give them a 20-dollar bill, a 1-dollar bill, and 42 cents and ask for change. You have taught the child that they don't have to end up with a wallet load of change every time they pay cash for something. Both of you can think up what something costs and how either of you would pay for it with the money on the table that would require some change back.

These games don't require a calculator and teach the child to think independently, making math fun.

If you successfully make this fun, your grandchildren will clamber to play it whenever they visit you or you visit them.

The next time you take the child to a fast-food restaurant, ask them what bills and change they would use to pay for their order before you hand over your plastic card to the cashier.

Of course, you can start with the little ones by having them match money to value. Check out our placemat at www.cjcorki.com/shop, or create your own.

Lifelong learning. What memories. What could be better? Play the Money Game and find out.

I was perplexed by how many young people working retail or fast food don't know how to change without what the computerized cash register tells them. They get completely confused when you give them $20, a $1, and 42 cents for a bill that comes to $6.42. In a somber tone, one young girl said that I gave her the wrong amount of money and was giving me my $20 back and said I gave her a $20 bill and not a $5 one.

Let's ensure our grandkids can do better. If you have any money-counting games or ideas, we'd love to hear them. Let's raise financially competent children together.

Put Your Hands-In-Your-Pockets Grandparenting

As a grandparent, you are most likely willing and eager to share your financial success. But part of raising capable children and grandchildren is to let them fail. With failure, they will learn.

"Helicopter Parent" is a term used to describe parents who constantly monitor their children's actions and decisions. Similarly, "Bulldozer Parent" is a parenting style where parents actively remove obstacles from their child's path, which can hinder their independence and ability to cope with adversity. This can apply to grandparenting, too. However, have you ever heard of "Hands-In-Your-Pockets" Grand-parenting? We coined this term to remind grandparents that you shouldn't give cash to your grandchildren without meaning or purpose. Instead, keep your hands in your pockets and see what lessons can be taught to the rising generation.

When our boys were little, we often visited the Jelly Belly factory outside Chicago. You were right on the floor with the candy-making process at that time. Our guide would state the number one rule, "Don't touch or take anything." Since most kids might be tempted to swipe a sweet toasted marshmallow or tutti-frutti bean, our guide suggested that the kids put their hands in their pockets to avoid temptation. So our advice to grandparents, even though you are tempted to give your grandchildren whatever they want, is to take a minute with your hands in your pockets to ponder a life lesson to be learned.

My parents gave my kids everything they couldn't get at home, like soda, ice cream, hotdogs, rice crispy treats, and Jello. That is fine; spoil them with unique delights. That isn't what I am talking about here. When children are financially given things, like asking for money or expensive items, they should be working or saving to buy.

My parents always gave the boys a fifty-cent piece when they visited. These were real silver coins dated 1969 or earlier. But the lesson was not to spend it on candy or gum; these valuable coins were to be saved for the future. They learned not only about coin collecting but also about delayed gratification and the value of savings.

"But I want it!" It might be the reason your three-year-old grandchild gives for getting a new toy. Or, "Everyone has designer purses" could be something your teenage grandchild says. When asked what they want this year, they say, "I want to go to Paris for my 16th birthday." When considering what to do, put your hands in your pocket and think about what lesson can be taught here.

Remember, it isn't about the money. Sure, you worked hard and could afford all of these easily. But now they need to learn that money doesn't grow on trees. If the three-year-old wants a toy, do they have skin in the game? What can they contribute to the payment? Might they have a piggy bank, birthday money, or extra chores they can do to earn money? If you are visiting with them for a couple of days, go home from the store and see about a plan to earn at least part of the toy.

Maybe they agree to pay half if they can earn the other part. Chores like feeding the dog, making their bed, and picking up toys are all things a three-year-old can do easily. But don't reward them extra if they already do that daily. Get creative, but within reason. Our son was three when he opened a lemonade stand. He made the sign, but I helped with the spelling. I also helped him make the lemonade, but he set the price. A quarter for a cup since he knew his coins, it was easy.

It also could be a lesson on charity. If the youngster wants a new truck and already has 10 of them, which one would he select to give to a needy family? The same goes for teenagers who wish to buy a new designer purse. Ask what clothes, shoes, or purses they want to donate.

When giving a big gift like a trip, it is essential to set boundaries. Simply planning the trip and expecting the recipient to show up doesn't teach any financial lessons. To ensure a good example, have the recipient organize it so that they can see what everything costs. You can set a budget, and they can decide where to spend it. Finding out why the destination is essential to them is also vital. They may find that their desired location didn't fit their budget or wasn't necessary to them. It is possible that they just thought it would sound cool to their friends.

My parents volunteered to take their grandchildren on a trip to spend time with them and make memories. This was a grandparent's weekend when the grandkids were about thirteen.

Each one would get a special weekend with Grandmother and Grandfather at a place of their choice. Some thought big, like New York City or Disney, while others thought smaller and more local. Those trips are unique, one-time trips and memorable times. Maybe too young to plan it, but still having some guiding principles and asking, "Why is the destination important?" In this case, a budget for daily expenses is reasonable. Rather have a souvenir than that dessert, sure. They were learning to make choices in a world of overindulgence.

If you just became a first-time grandparent or have not yet had any, this is a great time to consider becoming a "Hands-In-The-Pocket" grandparent. What lessons do you want to pass on regarding money? Remember, it is easier to plan than to play triage in the midst of "But I want it." But don't worry if you have that twenty-something grandchild; you still have a chance to inspire your fiscal lessons. Just keep your hands in your pockets.

Financial Capital Conclusion

Money is the first form of Capital, but it should not be the be-all and end-all of teaching about wealth. The famous quote from Benjamin Franklin, "Time is Money," should be reflected upon. Isn't spending time with your grandchildren the most important thing? Besides money, what would you like to pass on? What knowledge have you gained over your lifetime, and would you like to leave it with the rising generation?

Financial Capital
Bingo

This game is designed to integrate discussions about money and financial decisions into conversations with your grandkids. Mark off the squares as you complete each financial topic with them. The real "win" is learning about finances in a fun and interactive manner.

Open a bank account	Save for something specific together	Count Change	Find a penny on the street	Make a budget
Tell what you would do with $50.00	Buy a piggy bank	Read a kids book about money	Make a meal instead of going out to eat	Demonstrate with coins how interest works
Ask what they would do with $50.00	Play a money game	CJ CORKI	Create a family money jar	Turn off the lights & talk about savings
Make a money goal chart	Buy one share of stock	Research one stock together	Go to different stores and compare the price of eggs	Explain a bank statement
Buy gas and talk about the price per gallon	Pretend price everything in your bedroom	Gift $5.00 and guide them how to spend it	Play store, pay with cash and make change	Ask Alexa "what is money"

FINANCIAL CAPITAL ACTIVITY

Goals

What specific financial educational goals do you aim to provide for your grandchildren to support their future success?

Books:

- The Hen In The Pen by Paige Cornetet

- A Dollar for Penny by Julie Glass

- Alexander, Who Used to Be Rich Last Sunday by Judith Viorst

- Name Your Favorite: _____

Questions to Ask:

- What is money?

- If you had some money, what would you do with it?

- What does it mean to save money?

- Do you know why it's important to save some money for later?

Chapter 2

Intellectual Capital: The Role of Grandparents in Strengthening Family Bonds

Knowledge is only useful if you do something with it.

Jeffrey Pfeffer

Intellectual Capital Introduction

In the evolving landscape of the 21st century, Intellectual has never been more crucial. As we delve into this section on Intellectual Capital, we explore the vital role we, as grandparents, play in preparing our grandchildren for the complexities of the modern world. Intellectual Capital, the wealth of knowledge, creative thinking, imagination and innovative potential within each of us, is the cornerstone of our grandkids personal and professional success. With each of our rich tapestry of experiences and wisdom, we are uniquely positioned to guide our grandchildren in cultivating this invaluable asset.

Through our personal stories of both successes and failures that we have experienced, as well as lessons learned, we can impart critical thinking skills, foster creativity, and instill a love for lifelong learning. Let's help our grandkids lean into discomfort.

Crafting Tomorrow: The Journey to Building a Computer or Not

Let's start with a journey that began back in grade school. Along the way, there were moments of progress and personal growth that expanded the author's Intellectual Capital and helped to grow and improve her knowledge and skills.

Growing up in the 1970s, I dreamed large with Big Harry Audacious Goals (BHAG). During this computer age, Steve Jobs was changing the world in the personal computing industry. I wanted to be part of that. Intel, Xerox, and IBM were already making groundbreaking strides in the industry, but it was Steve Jobs who had a vision. A vision for everyone to have a personal computer in their home, which seemed absurd at the time. Who knew personal computers were only a piece of the puzzle of him changing the world? He was an inspiration.

In elementary school, we had Science Fairs, which I embraced wholeheartedly. My dad, the father of five girls, encouraged us to pursue the sciences. His mantra was, "Girls and boys are not equal; girls are better." I'm unsure if he was meant in general or the sciences, but I became passionate about learning as much as possible in this technical era.

My choice of a science project was building a calculator. In our basement, I spent hours with my dad soldering and assembling. But I was more interested in how it worked. The simplicity of the binary code was more up my alley. For those unfamiliar with it, binary is a system where a number is represented using only two digits (0 and 1) with a base 2. Simply, it is math, and that was my passion.

Yes, it was geeky of me. In elementary school, teachers would allow me to work ahead of the math curriculum. Racing through the problems, I was rewarded for my efforts with a prize. This excited me even more: the award, math puzzles. While the class was still learning the day's topic, I would be leaps and bounds ahead of what they were working on. It was more structured in high school, so I couldn't just work at my own pace. However, I did my homework while the teacher was still teaching the concept and then I helped any peer who needed assistance.

My initial major in college was none other than mathematics. But my dad asked me if I wanted to teach, which I did not. He suggested Electrical Engineering (EE), so I applied and transferred to Georgia Tech. And as they say at Tech, you cannot spell gEEk without EE. Little did I know that my dad's mantra was not correct. To my amazement, I was the only girl in most of my classes. Ignorance is bliss since I didn't know the statistical curve about males ranking higher than females in math.

But I marched on, studying long hours and trying my hardest to beat the curve. Much to my dismay, everyone wanted to go into EE for the same reasons I did: build computers. But the classes back then spanned the spectrum of curricula, not just relating to computers as they do today. I knew the material! I could do the long calculations but often missed simple algebra like 2+2. But there was no such thing as partial credit at Tech, which I depended on for most of my life. I would get the concept but make silly mistakes. Did you miss a negative sign? No credit. The teachers said that would be an upside-down bridge. UGH!

Okay, Georgia Tech beat me up and spit me out. When my classmates worked on voice recognition and automated voices (pre-Alexa), I knew this was beyond me. I was among people like Jobs who introduced his computer by having it say, "Hello." My EE friends would say things like, "I want to make a difference," or, like Jobs, "I want to change the world." And all of them were crazy enough to do it.

So, my first place in the science fair propelled me into the world of technology. Did I love it? Yes. Did I hate it? Yes. But my experience allowed me to work on some of my core values: perseverance. You might ask, "But you got out of EE?" I did, but I wasn't going to let the experience win. I gained a great deal of focus and attention to detail. I am also not afraid to try new technology and fail. My current quotation is, "I don't understand it, yet." Besides, one of my proudest moments was walking across the stage to receive my diploma. I believe that was my parents' too, grandkids aside.

As I go through life, I realize that I am no Steve Jobs and never would be him. In fact, after reading the biography, "Steve Jobs," he doesn't even live up to what is important to me: Family, Integrity, Perseverance, and Knowledge. Okay, maybe Knowledge, but he wasn't a nice person for most of his life. But he was an inspiration to a generation. Who or what inspires you? Who will you inspire?

As you can see, the world of binary numbers, is one type of knowledge but the arts and feeding our thirst for another creative outlet keeps Intellectual Capital alive.

Brushing Through Childhood: Memories from Art Lessons

Move over Picasso, Rembrandt, and Jackson Pollack. The next "master" of the arts is me...not.

As an adult, I learned to appreciate art, the lines, the strokes, the shading, and the visual stories that an artist tells, but let me take you back in time to how it was determined that my calling was not the world of paintbrushes and canvas.

Let me take you on a little trek down memory lane. In the 60s and 70s, filling every hour of a child's day with supervised activities wasn't necessary. Instead, it was a time when homework and chores were done, and playing with friends in the neighborhood until dusk was the usual way to fill our evening hours. Yes, we did periodically have activities, such as playing tennis in the street and Girl Scouts, but usually, that was as far as our orchestrated activities went.

You and I both know now that as we became adults, we realized that our parents used an extensive decision tree to deal with everyday living, throwing raising kids into the mix and quadrupling those decision points. But as kids, we didn't know what we didn't know. For example, I never even thought about the conversations our parents had about our health, their parenting style, or even the activities they thought would "round us out." But those thoughts occurred.

It was during one of those "rounding out" discussions one night that appeared to have brought one of those decision tree discussions that took the three eldest siblings into the world of "the arts." Piano lessons, tap and ballet lessons, and what is a robust "arts" education without art classes? Miss Tews, a tall, lanky, gray-haired 90-year-old woman, was the master of all these individual activities. We were fortuitous (?) enough to have back-to-back piano lessons once a week, be part of the group dance lessons, and finally, the chance to learn how to draw. She was the renaissance woman in Waukegan, Ill.

The logistics of mom working a full-time job, other family responsibilities, and now schlepping us to and from classes found us all taking the classes together. After all, we were all novices with no previous lesson among us...we were all the same, right?!

The three classes were held in the same studio on different days, so the studio smelled like a mixture of sweat and paint fumes. The sounds of the paintbrushes on canvas or the twinkling of piano keys from the class before us wafted the halls.

So, let me unlock the secret magic hidden in every swirl and swoosh of my childhood artistic escapades! I had none. I am sure we painted more than one picture, but the one that stays vividly in my memory is a landscape of wintery white hills, a house on the horizon, and kids sleighing down a hill. I combined my colors, dug into my inner memory of snow and fun, and created a duplicate of the sample picture that we were working from. My eldest sister, however, saw much, much more. She saw more than the picture in front of us. She painted a depiction of cherubic happy children, a warm fire waiting eagerly inside for the outdoor adventurers, and snow that enveloped you as you felt the picture take you to another place and time.

My eldest sister was a creative explorer. Beyond the technical skills she learned, she found a valuable opportunity for self-expression. She waltzed through all these classes armed with ballet slippers, paintbrushes, and even her sheet music, and she was fueled with natural artistic wisdom that took her outside the instructions. I believe that these lessons in "the arts" played a significant role in shaping her creative abilities and fostered a lifelong appreciation for art. I often asked her why she never practiced during our off times while I practiced until my feet or fingers were numb. She responded that she just "saw it."

The unintended consequences of putting us all in the same classes showed me that my talents were not my sisters and, at first, made me feel untalented and lacking on so many levels. However, there is a good side to this group venture. The memories and experiences with each brush stroke or pencil mark is where I learned that I can never compare myself to someone else but rather embrace my failure as a steppingstone toward improvement. I enhanced my problem-solving skills and critical thinking abilities and even pushed myself to look outside the box I put myself in.

The lesson this story teaches is that each child is different, and our job as parents is to unravel the talent of each of our children, foster their individual creativity, and plant the seeds for lifelong learning.

Let's help each child understand the wonder that each canvas held, turning ordinary days into extraordinary memories. Oh, and my sister and I visit art museums often, each with a different appreciation for the masters. Did she ever take an art class again? No, but the art of spinning, belly dancing, and theatre has been an integral part of her life.

We explored the depths of self-discovery through the canvas of art and the beauty in embracing new experiences. However sometimes the lesson is in the day-to-day joy in guiding our grandchildren through the kitchen, where trying something new becomes a delicious adventure.

You Know...it's all about the Little Things

So, guess what? My granddaughters came over to hang out with me for a whole four days! You won't believe how happy it made me when they both got super excited about cooking. My older granddaughter has cooked with me before, but this was the first time my younger granddaughter wanted to join in on the fun, too!

Always willing to whip something up in my kitchen, my little granddaughter and I started off by making pimento cheese for our yummy sandwiches for lunch. Since I like to make it from scratch (a Southern specialty), my granddaughter needed to shred the brick of cheddar cheese and drain the chopped jar of pimentos. I handed her the cheese block and the grater, and she started moving the cheese back and forth instead of up and down, clearly unaware of how to use it properly.

Engineering moment here--She had never seen a cheese grater before. Hmmm. I explained to her how cheese is shredded by running the brick over the sharp protruding part of the grater. Mission accomplished. I also watched to ensure that she didn't shred her knuckles/fingers when she was down to the nubs of the cheese brick. The last thing I wanted was a run to urgent care and having to explain bloodied knuckles to the attendant.

But I digress...

Next, find the colander. Simple? I asked her to get the colander from the cabinet. I pointed to the cabinet. She opened it and just looked perplexed. Clearly, she had never encountered a colander before. I took the chance to enlighten her. I pointed it out, and she readily got it down. We drained the liquid from the pimentos. She now knows what a colander is. It may seem like a small accomplishment, but to me, it signifies another success in the journey of learning and discovery.

It was finally time to make the pimento cheese. Note: This is a mix of pimento cheese, shredded cheddar cheese, and good ol' Dukes mayonnaise (because, well, we're down South). Then came the moment of truth – how to mix everything together. She began by mashing the mix. I stepped in and showed her how to scoop and fold the mixture to thoroughly mix it to get that perfect blend. I put my hand over hers and guided her through the process of how to fold ingredients together.

We then enthusiastically toasted the bread, adding a touch of warmth and crispiness that would perfectly complement our exquisite pimento cheese spread. She smeared the creamy cheese onto the bread with great care and attention to detail, creating mouth-watering sandwiches that would inevitably win over the most discerning palates, or so I thought.

The pimento cheese was seriously impressive, but when I gave my little granddaughter the sandwich, she flatly refused to even take a bite of the sandwich. To my surprise, she had never had a pimento cheese sandwich before and just wasn't interested in trying it out. I guess she's still in the chicken nuggets phase – kids.

It was disheartening, but I remain hopeful that one day, she'll willingly expand her culinary horizons and realize the fantastic flavors she's been missing out on.

As grandparents, we often don't realize how much our grandkids might not know. So, when planning a grandparent day or week visit, keeping some of the fundamentals in mind is essential. Kids are like sponges, and they're eager to learn new things, even if it seems like regular stuff to us.

They really do crave guidance and supervision. Spend a few minutes and think about the little things you do as part of your daily life, like washing dishes after a meal, making your bed in the morning, doing laundry, and sweeping the kitchen floor. These may have become a habit for you over the last 50+ years, but any and/or all these activities may be new experiences for them.

This isn't about throwing the parents under the bus. Realize parents are super busy and generally do this stuff themselves to save time, not often thinking about that children need to learn these activities too. That's where we come in, as grandparents! And remember to mix it up with some fun activities to help them take a break from their phone addiction. How about teaching them to cook, like making delicious pimento cheese together? They'll gain so much knowledge from it, and you'll get to bond with your grandkids in a meaningful way.

The Sound of Silence: Ghost Hunting in Notre Dame's Dark Stairwells

As we move into the haunting example of what limitless curiosity and creativity that evolved from our Intellectual Capital, we invented characters that will continue to haunt and influence.

Step with me into the shadows of history and architecture as we embark on a haunting journey to unravel the mysteries surrounding the legendary Ghost of Notre Dame. No, not the Notre Dame Cathedral in Paris where the infamous hunchback and monstrous gargoyles, silent witnesses to the supernatural, could be found, but rather the University of Notre Dame in South Bend, Indiana.

The hushed discussions about this prestigious school with high academic standards and rigorous programs were a grown-up conversation often heard after we were sent to bed.

One morning, we were suddenly faced with the statement that Mom and Dad would be taking the three eldest children to Notre Dame for the weekend. The questions swirled in our heads: why us?

What did we do right? Or what if there's something wrong that we did?

The 100-mile drive rolled on and on as the townscapes flew by, and anticipation and nerves wound together as we sat in the car, our hearts racing with a mix of anxiety and excitement, embarking on this new journey.

We discovered that this voyage had nothing to do with us but rather a marriage retreat for our parents. For those of you who don't know, a marriage retreat is an opportunity for couples to take a breather from their day-to-day activities and think about the marriage, share their experiences with others of the same faith, and reflect on their life.

While our parents were in workshops or group discussions during this retreat, we were housed in a dorm room. Perched atop a spiral staircase, the dorm room unfolded—a minimalist space adorned with three single beds and illuminated by a solitary light from overhead and a lone window at the end of the room.

Our responsibility was specific, "watch each other," "be good," and an additional explicit instruction to "stay in our room." Equipped with a diverse assortment of captivating books, we settled in our nook to immerse ourselves in our reading.

With the transition from daylight to dusk, a vast thunderstorm slowly approached, enveloping the surroundings in an impending atmosphere. As our gaze shifted from the pages of our book, we saw shadows and silhouettes stretching across the landscape. Intrigued, we succumbed to our curiosity, and the creaking of the door hinge led us into an expansive corridor lined with closed doors on either side, with a lone window beckoning at the end of the dimly lit hallway. Next to the window was another spiral staircase calling the three of us.

Now, picture yourself in this situation. What would you bring along? Perhaps your cherished and well-worn stuffed friend? A security blanket from years gone by? How about a trusty flashlight?

Not us; the sole object that caught our attention was a colorful, 12-inch round ball, and as we bounced it down the hall, the sound echoed off the walls. We discussed numerous topics among ourselves:

· What time was it?
· Why Mom and Dad weren't back yet?
· Why were there so many rooms and no sound coming from any of them?

Thump, thump, thump, the ball goes as the questions continue: what ghostly legends can be found in these dark walls? What if Mom and Dad were lost? When do we eat? Where does that lone staircase go?

With youth's boundless curiosity and imagination, we set aside our worries and queries. Playfully, we kicked the ball down the hall, tossing it back and forth. Then, one unnamed sister seized the ball and hurled it with the intensity of a dodgeball match. Though the dodge was successful, the ball tumbled relentlessly down, down, down the spiral steps, disappearing into the dark abyss below.

The collective gasps were palpable.

Oh no! Who's going to go down that dark stairwell? Our collective hearts were pounding at the speed of light. We linked arms as we slowly encouraged our feet to walk to the head of the stairs! Lions and tigers and bears, Oh my!! Strange noises and whispers emanated from the dark as if we awoke the monster below. They/it was alive as the lights started flickering and the hall was as cold as ice! We froze at the top of the stairs. Decision Time. Go! No, you go! Not me. We tried pulling rank, discussed drawing straws, and even threatened to "tell mom!"

Finally, with the collective intelligence and skills of the trio, we focused on the single goal of "retrieval at all costs," the ball was as good as safely back in our room.

One stood guard against imagined foes, one took up the arms of verbal encouragement towards success, and the third walked slowly and gingerly down those spiral stairs, the feeling of the cold, hard floor beneath the feet while walking down the spiral staircase to retrieve the lost ball.
Returning to our room with exhilarating triumph, we were relieved that the mischievous spirits hadn't relinquished their hiding spots. Armed with newfound wisdom, we realized that not even the enduring allure of the ghosts of Notre Dame could overshadow us when we united as a team of superheroes.

I believe that Mom and Dad's fateful retreat offered them the experience they were looking for. They learned the importance of teamwork and family bonds...and so did we.

From the bustling energy of the kitchen to the simplicity of a stairwell and a ball, the journey of learning extends far beyond culinary adventures, encompassing every corner of our lives and sparking curiosity in unexpected places, with Intellectual Capital feeding our imagination and thirst for knowledge.

Dare to be Different: What do Jacob's Ladder, Eyeballs, and Mice Have in Common?

Like Thomas Edison, the fledging scientists in all of us can say, that we have not failed, but rather found 1000 ways to not to do something. That single attitude is what builds our Intellectual Capital.

So, the question above is not a game where players embark on a magical journey to help mice reach new heights by navigating a whimsical world filled with Jacob's Ladders and enchanted eyeballs. Nor is it a new Artificial Intelligence robot.

Rather, they are science fair experiments.

Science Fairs...this yearly event caused excitement, enthusiasm, dread, and everything. Once announced, the questions started swirling. Can I come up with a creative idea? Or worse yet, any idea? A unique science fair project can be the perfect opportunity to showcase my originality, critical thinking, and problem-solving skills. If I opt for a conventional project, will it leave an impression on the judges to set me apart from the competition? Ugh, then there is: Can I find all the material? What is the purpose? Do I have the time to complete it? I was determined to make an impression on judges and visitors, so it was time to dare to be different!

Little did we know that we were learning outside-the-box thinking with the ability to design and execute a project on time and on budget and manage all the risks along the way. We were project managers before we knew what PMI* was!

Science fairs of the past, and even those of today, are excellent platforms for young minds to showcase creativity and innovation. So, how did we come up with such diverse ideas? Of course, it wasn't as easy as going to the internet and typing in "science fair ideas," which is less than a nanosecond; you can get a plethora of ideas by age, grade, and complexity. We relied on the Dewey Decimal system at the library and the magazine Popular Mechanics, which occasionally included hands-on DIY projects and science topics to create our "winning" experiment.

In retrospect, even though the front end of finding a project was more difficult for us than the current generations, what has remained constant is that the hands-on responsibility has stayed the same. The ideas are only the beginning; the execution and delivery can't be Googled.

So, what did I do? How about the influence of color on our appetites or a project that probes into the correlation between phases of the moon and human behavior? Hmmm, in the 1960s, the psychological influence on food wouldn't have even been "a thing." What about forensic science, combining forensic techniques on meat? It's a novel and unique angle for a science fair project my daughter created in the 1990s. Forensics research was my daughter's science project since NCIS wasn't a popular TV show in her era.

For me, I ended up with the Eyeball. Yes, my blood, sweat, and tears went into detecting eye issues, and I earned a 3rd place ribbon for my effort. The other two innovative ideas belonged to my oldest, who mastered the Jacob's Ladder, and sister #4, who was measuring how the eating habits of mice affected their longevity.

Are all science projects perfect? No way. Brimming with excitement, I presented my Eyeball to the judges; suddenly, there was an unexpectedly unleashed fury. Bam! Lava, once contained within its mountain, is now splattered everywhere. Everyone left their exhibits and ran into the commotion. My friend stood there covered from head to toe in "bubbly foam."

As I turned the corner, I saw my scientist friend's face move from shock to a chuckle. The absurdity of the volcano's untimely eruption demonstrated a valuable experience for all of us who witnessed the misadventure. Even in failure, there is room for growth, laughter, and understanding that things don't always go according to plan in the world of science and in life.

As grandparents, we can help support our grandkids in embracing the spirit of scientific exploration, where each attempt, whether successful or otherwise, fuels their understanding and curiosity about this wonderful world we live in. After all, science isn't just about significant discoveries—it's also about questioning, learning, and daring to be different.

My grandson isn't old enough to participate in a science fair...yet, but it's never too early for a bit of science. It not only helps in developing a deeper understanding of scientific concepts but also teaches success and failure. Try creating slimy worms or making non-Newtonian fluid. Age should never be an obstacle. To stand out from the competition and garner recognition, daring to be different. I didn't understand this as a kid, but I learned that the journey toward winning a science fair is not solely about the destination but also the process. The skills I acquired during the projects, such as critical thinking, problem-solving, and effective communication, were invaluable. I never became a professional scientist, but my sister, who created the Jacob's Ladder, did.

So, help your grandkids dare to be different and remember that regardless of the outcome, they should be proud of their efforts and recognize the invaluable skills they will develop during the process.

The next time you have the opportunity to gear up for a science fair, remember - your unique idea might earn you that desired recognition, if not a 3rd place ribbon!

From the escapades of the daring realm of science experiments, we continue to tell stores that move us to the pursuit of knowledge that perseveres, urging us to embrace failure on the path to understanding and discovery.

*Project Management Institute

The Magic of Museums: Making Memories with Grandma and Grandpa

Educating and inspiring visitors is the magical skill that museums bring.

My husband is a historian, and I'm a museum freak. We both will visit any museum we can find when we travel. We are using our passion with our grandchildren. Granted, many school groups visit museums through their schools, but when you have 30+ kids running through a museum, there is no real quality time with each exhibit, nor is there any context into what they are seeing. They have check-off lists. Did they see a duck? Did they see an ancient coin? It may be a fun scavenger hunt for the kids, but how much information do they retain? And there is no context.

This is where grandparents come in. A trip to the museum with grandparents is more leisurely; the kids don't need to return to the bus in an hour. And grandparents can embellish what the placards tell about the exhibit and interact with their grandchildren, asking what they see and think the exhibit is about and how they feel about it. This is an excellent opportunity for grandparents to put on their storytelling hats. These interactions are not available for the 30+ kids' school trips.

Most of us are not experts on dinosaurs or insects (except knowing how annoying mosquitoes, gnats—in the south, and flies can be). I get that, but many young children don't understand that dinosaurs predate humans, and that the lifecycle of many insects is fascinating. Time in the past is a fundamental concept. Many young children don't know what the word 'past' means. They live in the now. Their past is gauged in days, not millions of years. This is our opportunity to fill in the gaps their school field drips don't cover. Granted, you may not be an entomologist, but discussing an insect's lifecycle based on what the placards are presenting is a great way to get a dialog of questions and answers going. Ask your grandchildren what they think about these various lifecycles. This will open their minds to becoming more inquisitive.

You have your grandkids for the weekend and suggest everyone visit a local museum. The kids say, "We've been there." Don't be deterred. Like above, they may have been there but have no context about what they saw. Here is your opportunity to provide a deep understanding of their life experience.

We had one of our granddaughters for a week, and my husband wanted to make sure we took her to some of our local museums. We went to Fernbank Museum in Atlanta. I hadn't been there in years. Yes, we walked through the dinosaurs, but when we got to the natural history of Georgia, my husband enhanced her experience with personal information about the animals and flora in South Georgia, where he grew up. She was enthralled with his dialog. Something she would never have gotten from a school trip and a check-off list. Unlike my husband, I also learned a lot since I am not from South Georgia.

Distract your grandchildren from their cell phones when you get home by asking questions about what they saw and what they thought and where to go online (Google) to find more information. And then follow up with questions that they need to research. Sit down with your grandchildren at their computer and look up information together about what they experienced at the museum and learn with them. Talk with them. Encourage them to learn more about what they saw. Start a new habit for them by teaching them how to research topics instead of letting them view TikTok videos that are automatically generated for them. All interaction with your grandchildren is priceless.

So, if you haven't taken your grandchildren to a museum yet, seize the opportunity and create a cherished memory that will last a lifetime.

Build their Intellectual Capital by exploring and expanding your knowledge regardless of the digital realm of that of history and cultures.

Intellectual Capital Conclusion

Our hope is that these stories inspire you to reflect on the knowledge and experience that you possess and seek out ways to share those treasure with your grandchildren. Remember, every conversation, every shared moment of curiosity, and every lesson imparted contributes to the vast reservoir of Intellectual Capital that will shape the minds and hearts of those who come after us.

How about we embrace the role of guardians and cultivators of Intellectual Capital, for in doing so, we not only enrich the lives of our grandchildren but also contribute to the enduring legacy of humanity's collective wisdom and creativity. Herein lies our greatest gift and our most profound responsibility.

Intellectual Bingo

Intellectual bingo is a game that introduces topics like education, creativity, and imagination into conversations with our grandkids. Check off the squares as you explore each topic together. The true "win" is discovering what makes each of us unique in a fun and interactive way.

Imagine what you will be when you grow up	Do a science experiment	List the ways you are creative	Learn a new word	Create a coloring book
Design the car of the future	Write a poem about nature	Learn 5 facts about your favorite animal	Build the tallest structure	Share a mistake you made and what did you learn?
Travel 5 miles away, what did you learn?	Share your favorite class in school	CJ CORKI	Build something new with Lego's	Learn about a different country
Read 5 new books and decide on your favorite	Learn how something works	Visit the museum of art	Write a short story	Create a work of art
Identify your favorite book and why	Invent something	Find something totally new to try	Create a new color	Read a story about an inventor

INTELLECTUAL CAPITAL ACTIVITY

Goals

How do you want to inspire your grandkid's academic interests?

Books:

- The Cat with the Crocked Tail: A Dance-It-Out_Creative Movement Story by Once Upon a Dance and Olha Tkachenko

- Learn Something by Leah Hirschorn

- Something about the New Kid by Michael N. Lawrence

- Name Your Favorite: _____

Questions to Ask:

- Can you draw a picture of something you want to create or do when you grow up?

- Can you tell me about a new thing you learned recently?

- What do you learn when you make a mistake?

Chapter 3

Human Capital: Cultivating a Culture of Health and Wellness

By far the best investment you can make
is in yourself.
Warren Buffett

Human Capital Introduction

A family's Human Capital comprises the physical and emotional well-being of its members, their ability to find fulfilling work, establish a positive sense of identity, and pursue happiness. When each member takes care of themselves, helps one another, and engages in activities they enjoy, the family becomes a powerful team capable of taking on any challenge and having fun together. This includes things like eating healthy, exercising, enjoying various hobbies, setting goals, and dreaming. Unlike the knowledge gained from Intellectual Capital, Human Capital is what we do to be physically and mentally healthy, including finding purpose. Sharing good habits with grandchildren by modeling good behavior and teaching them how they can do the same is part of building a strong family balance sheet.

Kid Goals: Nurturing Dreams, Fostering Growth

Start with goals, achievements, or priorities to begin developing Human Capital. It doesn't matter what they are called; everyone should have them. Yes, even young children. Maybe it is to have good grades or something as simple as making their bed, doing choirs, or trying a new food or activity. Generally, goals are created as part of a New Year's Resolution, but since most resolutions typically don't last a couple of weeks, you might need some techniques to help. The secret sauce ensures the why is discussed, especially if it is a goal inspired by a parent or grandparent.

Getting A's in class, especially math classes, was one of my goals growing up. My only desire was to please my parents rather than the grade itself, which was my why. Grade school didn't seem too much of an issue keeping my grades on track. It wasn't until High School that I was distracted by other activities and boys. Or was it because I was perplexed by my parents' double standard for my siblings, specifically my sister, who was three years older?

When we received our report cards, we would proudly bring the grades to my dad. He would sit in his rocking chair, smoking his pipe while he reviewed the reports. "Three A's and two B's?" he would say to me, "Can't you bring up the B's?" I was disappointed with my performance, which I had thought was pretty good before the encounter. But my sister would bring her report card with a different reaction, "Two Bs and three Cs. Did you do your best?" he would say. After responding with a yes, he would give her a "that's my girl" response.

Being the youngest in the family, you are assumed to be the "golden" child. You are believed to be spoiled by your parents and grandparents. Instead, I was one-upped by my older siblings. Not just my sister, who was closest to me in age and my dad's favorite, but the ones ten years older who were in the process of changing the role of being a woman in the 1960s and 1970s. They were breaking barriers in science and business. The first woman doing this, the first female doing that. How could I compete since I could only be second in those achievements? And I was already the fifth in the family.

"It took five times to get it right," my sisters would joke with me about being the youngest. I might not have been the first to do a lot of things, but it was instilled in me to be goal-oriented. When my husband and I had kids, we would do things differently. Having three children by the age of 30 was my first goal. That was highly aggressive since I didn't get pregnant with our first until I was 27. Strangers teased me about their young ages with comments like, "You know what causes that?" But they were all part of the plan.

Encouraging each of them to be their unique selves was another priority. However, without my help, they were born with different talents, and it was our job as parents to help them develop those skills. Regarding grades, we took the route I wished I received, "Did you give it your best?" I would ask. Maybe we were not challenging them enough, but with two of the three children having dyslexia, I was more concerned with mental health than the grades themselves.

"Make your bed," nope, that wasn't a goal for our children. Maybe I was worn down, but getting them out of that bed and to school was more of a priority than nagging them about an unmade bed. Besides, my parents never cared if I made my bed or not. They didn't make our bed either, and I didn't make my kid's bed; it was just left the way they rolled out of bed.

But as I matured into grandparenting age, I realized that they might have been more inclined to achieve the goal if I included the why about the goal. Why get good grades? Maybe it is the satisfaction of achievement or showing you are proficient in certain subjects. Why make your bed? Along the line of Admiral William H.

McRaven's commencement speech, when you start your day with the small things, it leads you to accomplish more significant things. And if you had a bad day, you have a nicely made bed to come home to.

The WHY is the key to any goal you want to achieve or what you are encouraging your grandchildren to achieve. Why save your money? My parents did make that point very clear: to save for college. In any job I ever had, I had to preserve, not spend, to save up for college. But are my parents or grandparents paying for college? Yes, mine, too. But it was the books, the apartments, and just being able to eat, which was not covered by my parents, that I needed money for. I even worked during college and still relied on that money so I wouldn't have the "food insecurity" you hear about today on campuses.

As a grandparent, what are some goals you have for your grandchildren? Make sure you understand the why. Check with the parents to ensure you are all on the same page. But realize that as a grandparent, specifically a grandmother, the influence you have. Research has proven that the most significant impact is on goal setting for their grandkids. Typically, they see potential before even the parents do. How are you going to inspire the next generation?

Junior Achievement: Fostering Human Capital for Business Success

Junior Achievement has long been recognized as a cornerstone in cultivating Human Capital, igniting the entrepreneurial spirit, and equipping young minds with essential skills for a dynamic future.

Growing up in the 1960s, I was a master player; by that, I mean playing Red Rover, tag, tennis, and all that kids do, running around in a carefree and safe life. But everything changed when, at the age of 13, I was recruited to become a superhero. Yes, an elite group known only as Junior Achievement was added to my life. Junior Achievement (J.A.) was a training ground for young minds, where kids could cultivate uncommon talents and fly into the world of business and economics!

Imagine a place where learning feels like a thrilling adventure, where kids can explore the ins and outs of entrepreneurship, money management, and real-world economics.
Our JA program expanded our traditional classroom learning. The learning model was engaging, and to this new enthusiast, it inspired me. Only years later, as an adult, I learned that the model was designed to "teach, touch and sell." "Teach, touch, and sell" is a business strategy that focuses on engaging the young mind in understanding how business works. The adults that ran the program were real business leaders. Ours came from Fansteel, a local manufacturing company. They first used "teach." By providing short snippets of educational content, they didn't make it feel like we were in school but did offer us insights into how companies work and what drives people to buy in a fun, interactive way.

During our session, we moved on to the "touch" part, where we were given a blank canvas to brainstorm ideas as a team and create a product we could sell. This hands-on activity allowed us to interact with each other and take our playtime to a new level. The final stage of our weekly meetings was focused on the "sell" aspect, where we spent time figuring out who our target audience was and how to convince them to buy our product. We shifted our focus from simply creating the product to ensuring it had a market and people would want to buy it. Although we secretly wondered if anyone would buy our product, we remained optimistic and worked hard.

By combining these three elements – teaching, touching, and selling – we also learned about the emotional side of selling. We had no baseline to understand if our product would sell, but we created an unexpected best-seller for the J.A. trade fairs. Psychedelic flowers.

Can you imagine that paper flowers took the top spot as the best-selling item at the J.A. Trade Fair? Twenty-five companies ran a J.A. program and sold at this fair. We sold out the first day and had to figure out how to keep this momentum going. So, we recruited our younger sisters and formed an assembly line in our family room as we mass-produced our large flower. From conflict came innovation, and we actually learned to pivot and create smaller flowers that could be produced quicker and diversify our product line. An unintended consequence was that we learned resourcefulness and to spot opportunities and execute seamlessly. Success.

Yes, through J.A., we learned the ropes of financial literacy, the ABCs of business, and the superpowers of critical thinking and problem-solving. It was not just about textbooks and lectures; it gave us hands-on experience by rolling up our sleeves and diving headfirst into developing our Human Capital, even though, at the time, we had no idea that we did.

J.A. helped us explore our interests, passions, and talents to set us up to ambitious goals for our future. Not to be forgotten how, it helped us build our confidence and learn that we do not have all the answers.

I will always wonder if our Junior Achievement experience was a planned strategy by our parents or if it was an opportunity that fell into their laps. Either way, to help our grandkids grow their Human Capital, let's help them find their "J.A." and encourage them to undertake something new. It will play a vital role in increasing their Human Capital by providing them with the knowledge, skills, experiences, and connections they need to succeed in the ever-changing world.

Remember, this is about more than just the young; show them that starting something new is never too late. It's also never too late to cultivate your own uncommon traits; how will you expand your Human Capital?

Success Stories: Thriving as a Non-Athlete in an Athletic World

Speaking of starting something new, I think of my mom, who "ran" the Marine Corps Marathon at 86 years old. Okay, she walked the 10K, but the Marines awarded her a full marathon medal. I was privileged to run the full marathon the same weekend my mom and sisters walked the 10K. We experienced the "something new" as a family.

Being part of the one percent who have completed a marathon is an incredible feat that demands unwavering determination, steadfast dedication, and thorough preparation. By committing to a consistent training schedule, maintaining a healthy lifestyle, and having the right equipment, I could conquer the physical and mental obstacles that come with the marathon distance. Despite encountering the infamous "wall," I emerged victorious; I finished.

When I returned home, drained and bone tired, my youngest son asked me if I won the race. He thinks winning first place is not just a participation medal for finishing. Although I felt a sense of accomplishment, I reflected on my many episodes in sports of not winning and not being an athlete.

My childhood was a complete failure in sports. I played volleyball, but more accurately, I warmed the bench. Unfortunately, I was one of the tiniest in my class. Not just because of genetics, I am still not tall, but also because I was almost a year younger than most classmates.

Completing with much older children, I didn't pass the Presidential Physical Fitness Test in elementary school, which awards children for their fitness achievements. When it was time to pick sides in dodgeball, I was the last chosen. But I would be the first to be called for "Red Rover,

Red Rover" since I could never break through the opposing lines.

I skied as I entered high school, which my parents taught me at five years old. But I enjoyed going slowly down the hill and doing some tricks along the way, nothing too daring. But my skills were put to shame on my first adventure to ski in Switzerland. Let's say the mountain won, and I limped away with a torn ACL.

In college, I had to take drown-proofing to graduate. Fortunately, the requirement changed, and I just had to begin swimming. I was the only girl in the class and was put with basketball players. I passed despite the teasing and graduated.

So, as our kids started coming along, I wanted to ensure they didn't endure that low confidence that comes from having no athletic abilities. From the age of 11 months, they had Gymboree class, which evolved into gymnastics. Swimming, yep, I couldn't save them with my poor swimming abilities, so they learned to swim at 3, 4, and 6 years old. Soccer, baseball, tennis, hockey, wrestling, rugby, basketball, golf, archery, fencing, cross country, lacrosse, skiing, and more were all sports they were exposed to.

Although, as their mother, I didn't play a significant role in making them into the talented athletes they are today. I endured the endless smell of dirty socks, pungent shin guards, and the ridiculously rank smell of a gym bag that was left at school all season.

While some might argue that nature vs. nurture is a factor, I would like to point out that their father, my husband, is also very talented in sports. We encouraged our children to try various sports, but we also didn't pamper them every time they stumbled or tried something new that we thought they weren't ready for, such as riding a bike without training wheels and skiing at three years old.

Today, raising an athletic child involves creating a supportive environment that promotes physical activity, skill development, and a healthy lifestyle. However, enticing them away from electronics might be the most brutal battle. Here are some ideas.

Encourage your child to engage in active play from an early age. Provide opportunities for them to run, jump, climb, and explore outdoors. Tag, hide-and-seek, and bike riding promote physical fitness and coordination. So they take their training wheels off at three years old; who cares if they are determined to learn?

Be a role model for your child by staying physically active and leading a healthy lifestyle. Children often emulate their parents' behaviors and attitudes. Even if it is a non-talent sport like my running, it shows that physical health is prioritized.

Expose your child to a variety of sports and physical activities. Let them explore different options to discover their interests and talents. But let your child be your guide. While our middle son was being twisted in a knot during a wrestling match, he looked at me and said, "Mommy, he is hurting me." Little did I know he would become a Ju Jitsu black belt as an adult.

Create a supportive and positive environment for your child's athletic pursuits. Please encourage them to enjoy the process of learning and improvement rather than solely focusing on winning. We were fortunate to have good coaches who concentrated on our child's development to be good men, not just to win at all costs.

Give your child opportunities for unstructured, free play where they can be creative and imaginative. But be careful what you wish for; this can lead to over-creativity. For example, our boys took their circle sleds down the basement stairs. They had a ball; Mom had a scare.

Remember that not every child will be an athlete, much less a one percenter, and that's perfectly fine. The primary focus should be promoting a healthy and active lifestyle, developing essential life skills through sports, and having fun. Look at me. I had no skills or obvious talent but made it into that elite category. Athlete or not, get moving! Model the healthy Human Capital traits of physical fitness and maybe try something new.

Crafting a Culinary Identity: My Selectatarian Journey

Although exercise is an important activity, so is nutrition. Despite my dad's attempts to convince me that it was okay for different foods on my plate to touch each other, I stood my ground and stuck to my personal preferences. This experience taught me to trust my instincts and not be swayed by others' opinions. Even before I knew the word's meaning, I was on a journey to become a Selectatarian, a personalized path to optimal nutrition.

When I was six years old, my favorite food was SpaghettiOs. For those who don't know, SpaghettiOs are a type of canned pasta that comes in a ring shape and is served with tomato sauce. They are marketed to parents as a "less messy" alternative to regular spaghetti. This meant the sauce wouldn't mix with my broccoli, making me cry whenever it did. If this happened, I would be sent to the stairs until I could calm down, which often meant missing dinner altogether.

Although canned food was my preferred choice, my Polish family used to make Polish sausage from scratch. I vividly recall the heavy grinder on the table churning out tubes of this supposed deliciousness. However, as a child, watching the process made me dislike the meat. Maybe mixing the fats and the meat into a tube triggered my aversion to food touching. But to this day, I avoid this food group entirely.

Blood soup, anyone? This soup has been a significant part of Polish culture for several centuries. It was traditionally served during marriage proposals until the 19th century. However, as a child, the idea of drinking blood like a vampire, even if it was just duck blood, was revolting. In my family, we have it every Christmas Eve, along with other traditional Polish dishes like pierogi and sauerkraut.

When I was a child, my diet often lacked nutrition. To address this, my mom would insist once a week that I eat liver and onions while the rest of my family dined on fried chicken. My sisters indulged in their tasty meal while I stared at my plate, hoping nobody would notice that I wasn't eating. If they did, I would move the food around my plate until they touched it, giving me an excuse not to eat it.

But my oldest sister, the chemistry student, sent me over the edge with my eating preferences. When she would come home from college, she would read the labels on the cans and explain to me what all those preservatives meant. Some ingredients included high-fructose corn syrup, artificial flavors and colors, and hydrogenated oils—no more SpaghettiOs for this child.

Then came the discussion on how they process hotdogs, bologna, and more. But it wasn't until the talk about the feed lots that I was able to break away from all meats. My sister, already a vegetarian, convinced me it was the way to go nutrition-wise. It wasn't to save the animals or the climate as discussed now; it was strictly a health decision, although taste had much to do with it.

Constantly challenged to get enough protein, I was reduced to consuming horse pill-sized chewable protein. High school and college cafeterias didn't meet my dietary preferences, so I lived on peanut butter and apples. It didn't take long to move from vegetarian to pescatarian; I introduced fish to my diet to get more protein.

So when we bought my husband's family's historic farm, we decided not to grow grapes or crops. We opted to raise cattle. It makes sense for a vegetarian turned pescatarian. Our cows aren't just run-of-the-mill cattle. We raise Wagyu, the genetics of the prized Kobe beef from Japan. The fat on consistency is remarkably different than Angus. It has a lower melting point and is considered a healthy fat. The Wagyu herd is raised right with no antibiotics or hormones, and they are free to roam the pristine rolling countryside and drink fresh spring water. They go from the "Field to the Fork." It cannot get fresher than that.

So, after 40 years of vegetarianism, I started to study nutrition. I discovered the importance of animal protein in the diet, such as essential amino acids, iron, omega-3, zinc, and more. With our cattle being raised well, I decided to try some. Wow! You would think my system would have an issue or I wouldn't like the taste. That's not true. I felt great after eating it, and it tasted amazing.

I used to think the "farm to table" movement was just a passing trend, but now I realize it's the healthiest way to eat. I have started my garden and plan to expand it by raising chickens. When I have grandchildren, I want to teach them about growing and raising their food so they can better understand where their meals come from. In today's world, many young people are disconnected from the source of their food, so I want to help them broaden their diets and develop a deeper appreciation for their food.

Today, I am still very particular about my food, sticking to what I believe. Although I still refuse to eat Polish sausage or Blood Soup, fresh Wagyu from our farm or Trout from our pond have become regular parts of my diet. I have recently discovered the term Selectatarian, which is not a common word; it has been used to describe a unique or personalized approach to eating. I eat fresh, clean, and right from the farm.

What do your grandchildren know about nutrition? Do they have a particular preference for canned spaghetti? It's important to avoid pushing unwanted foods on them. I recall my mother-in-law's attempt to make tofu cheesecake for her grandkids, but it didn't go well because it tasted terrible. However, it's helpful to encourage them to try new things and let them decide later if it's something they don't like after tasting it.

Are your kids aware that lettuce doesn't come from a bag and that chickens lay eggs? If not, consider starting a garden, raising some chickens, or taking them to visit a farm. There are countless ways to make healthy eating enjoyable and in doing so, you'll also be promoting good mental health.

Lifting Small Boats: Being Mentally Wealthy

What is a growth mindset? Happiness is a part of the Human Capital equation. Adopting a growth attitude will bring happiness to you and future generations, and if you are happy, you are wealthy.

During a social studies class at my parochial elementary school, I first learned the history of Head Start. According to benefits.gov, "Head Start is a Federal program that promotes the school readiness of children from birth to age five from low-income families by enhancing their cognitive, social, and emotional development." Wow, it hit me; our family must have been poor since I went to Head Start. I never felt poor. My sisters and I had pretty dresses, black patterned leather shoes, and fancy hats to wear to church on Sunday. I was never hungry, although the food quickly disappeared from the refrigerator since we were a family of seven. My family was part of a family business, so I started working as soon as I could walk. I earned all the money I could need and saved it, too. My parents taught us about tithing, which was demonstrated by their weekly checks to the church. So, what does being poor mean?

Consistently, the Census Bureau reports that more than 30 million Americans are considered poor. According to the government's data, "the average American family or single person, identified as poor by the Census Bureau, lives in an air-conditioned, centrally heated house or apartment that is in good repair and not overcrowded. They have a car or truck. The home has at least one widescreen TV connected to cable, satellite, or streaming service, a computer or tablet with an internet connection, and a smartphone. According to their report, the average low-income family had enough food throughout the prior year. No family member went hungry for even a single day due to a lack of money for food." This scenario sure doesn't sound like what the media portrays as crime-ridden, drug-infested homeless camps. Although homelessness is genuinely a problem from my research, it just isn't the norm for those classified as poor. The government defines poverty as if "money income" lies below a certain threshold, not homelessness.

With that definition, maybe my family was poor. We didn't have air-conditioning, widescreen TVs, or Smartphones, but that was because of the era, not from the level of wealth. Our family also had the support of grandparents and relatives. My aunt always offered us a fifty-cent piece when we visited or food from the family store—the family business allowed for pretty dresses, shoes, and hats. My grandparents also drilled the idea that if you went to college, you would be successful; otherwise, you would be on the streets as a homeless bum—pretty strong words from grandparents who only had a high school education. But even though we were poor mentally, we considered ourselves wealthy. We went to private schools and graduated from college. It wasn't a poor mentality, but one with the mantra, "The World is Yours."

My grandparents came from Poland, which was not a land of opportunity back then. They came to America because they knew it could be a better life for themselves and their families, and it was. They started a family business where, even through the Great Depression, they could feed their family. They struggled to succeed, but their Pursuit of Happiness, much like the movie, didn't have a poverty mindset.

While living in a free country pursuing their dreams, they felt obligated to Lift Small Boats back in Poland. The concept is that if you help those struggling financially, everyone benefits. My family would sew U.S. dollars into the hems of clothing and send it to relatives in Communist Block Poland. U.S. cash at the time could get you goods that weren't available with Polish currency. They also assisted other family members in relocating to America to pursue their ambitions. As a close neighbor, now the Ukrainians need our help to fight back against the same powerful country, Russia.

Throughout my childhood and into adulthood, the lessons my parents taught me I would like to introduce my grandkids. Work hard, have a growth mindset, and believe in yourself. But more than anything, consider the "World Is Yours" and "Lift Small Boats Along the Way."

Unleash Your Inner Renaissance Genius: Inspiring a Young Polymath

Developing hobbies and interests is part of personal growth. Prioritizing exercise, nutrition, and mental health are essential to a positive and growth mindset.

During the Renaissance period from the 14th to the 17th centuries, individuals with a wide range of intellectual, artistic, and practical skills were known as "polymaths" or Renaissance men. These people were admired for their diverse talents, broad knowledge, and ability to excel in multiple areas of expertise. A Renaissance man was expected to understand several subjects, such as literature, philosophy, mathematics, science, art, music, and more.

How do we inspire the next generation of Polymaths? Growing up in a small Polish community, the far-reaching identity of a Renaissance Man or, in our case, a woman, was too far from reality. Although I don't claim that distinction, my parents encouraged many hobbies.

We always worked at our family business, which meant we had disposable income at a young age. Since my parents covered food, clothing, and shelter, after we contributed to our college savings, we had leftover money for random expenses. I spent some of the money on buying plaster figurines.

Plaster figurines came in various themes, such as animals, flowers, and fairy tale characters. Most were small, but we occasionally purchased one close to a foot tall. The shop was within walking distance from our house, so my sister and I would walk up to make our selection. I was about eight years old when I was passionate about this hobby.

Coin collecting evolved from our family store. As we worked the cash register, we spotted Wheat Pennies quickly. But we also eyed the coveted 50-cent piece, which before 1970 was made of silver. But coins from the Liberty nickel to a steel penny were entered into our treasure trove of coins. My dad and I would spend hours cleaning them and arranging them in coin books, which I still have today.

My sisters played the piano, which I napped to as a baby. Mozart, Chopin, and other classics would lull me to sleep. Although I listened to their artistic abilities, my lessons didn't go as well. I tried, but it was a short-lived experience. I plan on correcting that now that I am an adult.

Our science experience evolved with the endless science fairs my sisters participated in. Jacobs Ladder, fighting cocks, and mice experiments, to name a few, that my sisters and, subsequently, I were involved in. I was an observer and sometimes a participant, but the lessons learned were inspiring to become hobbies or activities I also enjoyed.

My parents always encouraged reading. In the summer, we would walk to the public library to choose our books for the week. We would log the books we read for a reading award. Although I was an early reader, I enjoyed math more than books. However, my oldest sister gave me the Lord of the Rings books, which I devoured. I am still a voracious reader of all genres.

Philosophy in our family was always religious. It wasn't until college that the two merged. The question asked, "If you say you are an atheist, you are saying you don't believe in God, so you are in reality saying God exists." Wow, it blew my mind. Philosophy was a passion, very mathematical, "if that, then this."

However, learning a language has been a constant failure. My parents spoke Polish at home, but I never picked it up. Even after formal Polish language classes, I only have a basic one or two-sentence understanding. In high school, I took two years of French only to be able to say the "Hail Mary" in French. I studied in the Italian section of Switzerland only to get a D in Italian. Not my forte.

But inspiring the rising generation seems to be easier than perfecting my list of skills. Our son, who aims to become a Renaissance Man, is realizing that. He has an engineering degree from Virginia Tech, where he was an athlete and a lacrosse player. After graduation, he became a rock climber, climbing Kilimanjaro. He became a scuba diver and surfboarder in Australia. He is striving to become a black belt in jiu-jitsu. His ballroom dance skills have been rated high in competitions. He has been learning Czech and Russian to communicate with friends and colleagues.

So, how do we inspire the rising generation to develop hobbies? First, be an example of a growth mindset and keep learning. Second, encourage any interest a child might have. If a boy wants to take ballet, fantastic. Suppose a girl wants to be a bull rider, excellent. Even hobbies you might not necessarily think are beneficial, check your bias and open your mind to inspiring a young polymath.

Human Capital Conclusion

Building your family's Human Capital requires setting goals, achieving them, and finding purpose. Encouraging creativity in your grandchildren can help with this. However, Human Capital also includes taking care of your health by staying active with exercise, sports, and movement, such as walking. Good nutrition is also important for maintaining good fitness. Additionally, it's crucial to prioritize your grandchildren's mental health. Lastly, when teaching your grandchildren about a growth mindset, encourage them to explore new hobbies and interests. Remember, the way they interact with others is also important, as this is part of our next chapter, Social Capital.

Human Capital
Bingo

This bingo facilitates discussions about a family's human capital. This includes activities such as taking care of oneself physically and mentally, assisting each other, and pursuing passions, all while being prepared to tackle any challenge. As you engage in these activities, mark off the squares to track your progress. The actual "victory" lies in developing this essential life skill through enjoyable and engaging activities.

Make and complete a goal for the week	What do you want to improve about yourself?	Exercise 1 day with your parents	Empty the dishwasher	Play "Simon Says"
Learn how to say hello in 3 different languages	Play follow the leader	Share your favorite dream	Who do you admire? Why?	Exercise daily for one week…keep it going
Learn Pickleball	Watch a sporting event	CJ CORKI	Learn a new hobby	Learn a new sport
What is your favorite healthy food?	What are you most proud of?	What are you responsible for at home?	Eat a new fruit	Collect 10 coins with different years
What was your biggest mistake?	When is it hardest to be patient?	What is your wildest dream?	Make your bed everyday for a week	What do you do when you are sad?

HUMAN CAPITAL ACTIVITY

Goals

How do you plan to help them invest in personal development and well-being to contribute to their growth?

Books:

- Giraffes Can't Dance by Giles Andreae

- Oh the Places You Will Go by Dr. Seuss

- Eat Your Peas by Kes Gray and Nick Sharratt

- Name Your Favorites: _____

Questions to Ask:

- Are there any new skills or hobbies you would like to learn or improve?

- What do you do to stay physically active and healthy?

- What personal goals do you have for the next year?

Chapter 4

Social Capital: Enhancing Trust and Communication in the Family

Social capital refers to connections among individuals – social networks and the norms of reciprocity and trustworthiness that arise from them.

Robert D. Putnam

Social Capital Introduction

The quote succinctly captures the essence of Social Capital, emphasizing the importance of connections, networks, and the beliefs that bind individuals together in a family, community, and society. Facilitating the building and nurturing of these connections enhances communication, trust, and collaboration, which are vital for both personal and family success. Social Capital enriches the bonds by strengthening relationships, influencing the world around us, shaping our roles and family dynamics, reinforcing bonds, molding our behavior through interactions with each other, and extending those interactions even when separated by distance. Growing inwardly as a family and extending outwardly into the community broadens the familial influence on everything from individual well-being to societal global impact.

Growing Pains or Growing Bonds? How to Foster a Strong Family Connection in Adulthood

Building a relationship with family members is a top priority of Social Capital. However, growing up with siblings can be a wild ride.

In my family, we were all girls, with three sisters born a year apart and another two born five and ten years later. Talk about two families! Even with the age differences, we were all born in the baby boomer generation, which added to our being vastly different in every way imaginable. The only thing we had in common was sharing one bathroom. Growing up was far from easy.

Decades have passed, everyone scattered from our little local community, and the wild commonality and the time spent together became less and less. What do you do? The easy answer would be to move on with the new life we created as adults, with careers, spouses, children, and friends surrounding us, but we were always searching for the easy answer. Now, I would like to take credit for bringing the siblings back together, but my sage 4th sister, in 2003, said something so simple yet profound that it changed our adult lives forever.

How did it happen? It all began with an opportunity. Opportunities are woven into our daily lives. Some we choose to navigate, forging a new, unique journey, while others fleetingly pass us by. This change changed all our lives forever. Our oldest sister was living in D.C., I was in the Philadelphia area, our parents were in Chicago, and our sage sister #4 was in Atlanta. We decided to gather for a weekend in our state capital. We hadn't been together for years, and our short journey didn't have one defining moment, but we walked, ate, laughed, and talked.

As the weekend ended, out of the mouths of babes came, "This was great fun. Why don't we get all the sisters together and do this again? "...and the sisters' weekend concept was born.

Of course, the exhilaration of the moment and the "high" from the weekend had to be moved from vision to implementation. Mom and Dad had been "herding cats" our entire childhood, and now these "cats" were independent, opinionated adults. This job could have been daunting to others, but we never even thought about it not occurring. The three of us knew something was missing and believed everyone wanted to invest in our family relationship and would go the extra mile to nurture these connections as adults.

The successful execution of any project is in the details. It is no different when planning an adult weekend. If it's your first, like us, it began with "selling" the big picture on why gathering as sibling adults is essential.

Next. What are the rules of engagement? Open and honest communication is critical. In our case, we still must remind ourselves to actively listen to other opinions, especially if they see preferences differently. Compromise and understanding goes a long way.

What are we going to "do" during this time? The success of our 2003 event occurred because it was peppered with spontaneity, which led to unexpected discoveries. Even though it might sound like an oxymoron, the spontaneous time should be scheduled. The successes occur between the balance of relaxation and excitement. Create a loose itinerary.

Where to go and how often rounds out the planning. A few discussion points will naturally change by year, situation, and life. Is it a rotation between each other's homes and cities? Do we select a city somewhere else in the country? Do we alternate the coasts or even the Midwest? Is there a time of year that works best for everyone? My oldest sister is a sheep shearer, and the spring is off the table because that is when sheep are in desperate need of grooming. How about September? Another sister has a yearly national business meeting that must be considered. Schedules, calendars, and logistics we hadn't even thought of...easy, right?

The second tier of these events wasn't considered initially. Would we get along? In theory, our core bond and values should withstand any hiccup. Let's put it to the test, and so we did.

The journey is approaching its 20th anniversary. Evolution is necessary, and from our first event, it has morphed from sisters only to spouses. Even though some weekends have been emotional and challenging experiences, we have honed our conflict resolution and forgiveness skills. As we continue to evolve and grow, we have a solid support system and a sense of belonging that is hard to find anywhere else.

I share this story to equip you with valuable insights and practical advice for building your journey with your adult siblings.

Navigating the dynamics of family relationships in adulthood can be challenging yet immensely rewarding as we strive to maintain and strengthen our bonds with loved ones. As we work on fostering these connections, it's important to remember that small, seemingly mundane actions can profoundly impact our lives, the overall family, and the world around us.

One such simple yet transformative habit is making your bed each morning. This daily practice sets a positive tone for the day and reinforces a sense of discipline and accomplishment that can ripple through various aspects of life. Let's explore how this small act can contribute to personal growth (Human Capital) and make an impact on the world (Social Capital).

Making Your Bed: How it Can Change the World.

My mom always encouraged me to make my bed in the morning. But as a youngster, I always wondered what the point was. I woke up in the morning, left for school, came home, did homework, ate dinner, watched TV, and then went back to bed. Why make my bed when I return in the evening and unmake it again? Little did I know she was teaching me how to change the world.

You might wonder how this little task can make a difference. Frankly, I only understood it once I became an adult. Naval Adm. William H. McRaven, ninth commander of U.S. Special Operations Command, at the University-wide Commencement at The University of Texas at

Austin, said, "What starts here changes the world. If you can't do the little things right, you will never do the big things right." His inspiring message states that if you start by doing the little things, it motivates you to continue doing bigger and bigger tasks, leading to changing your life for the better as well as others. And if you had a terrible day, at least you can come home to a nicely made bed showing your first daily accomplishment.

In the commencement speech, McRaven said, "...find someone who can help you paddle." My parents, too, had a similar message but with a bit of a twist. They would say, "Friends will come and go, but family is forever." You can depend on family—someone who will support you through the good and bad times. They will be there when you need advice, a shoulder to cry on, or a sounding board to vent or brainstorm. I have been blessed with four sisters who have always been there for me.

Another message acknowledged in the speech is that you should measure a person by the size of their heart, not the size of their flippers.

Although this reference refers to physical size, which is not how you should be measured, the objective measure is hard work. Similarly, my parents gave us the same lesson. They said, "Don't measure someone by the size of their bank account, but how hard they work. Never marry for money, rather for their work ethic."

"If you want to change the world, get over being a sugar cookie and keep moving forward," McRaven explained that the punishment for not having your uniform in order as a Navy SEAL was a requirement to roll in the sand. I remember our punishment for not behaving was to scrub the entire front porch with a toothbrush. It gave us humility, but we moved on, knowing not to misbehave again.

McRaven said, "If you want to change the world, don't be afraid of the circuses." The circuses were a place of punishment where you would have to endure additional calisthenics, runs, and other physical hardships. They may have been difficult, but the circuses made you better. Although my parents didn't stress physical activity, they did stress achievement.

Sometimes, it took practice, long hours, and many failures before success. They encouraged me not to be afraid of it. Check out our intentional grandparenting book, Not My Circus.

"If you want to change the world, sometimes you must slide down the obstacle headfirst." My parents always encouraged me with a similar mantra to go into something wholeheartedly. "Just dive right in, why wait," they would say. I think of this lesson every morning. Why wait until later? Like Nike's tagline, "Just do it," my parents said, "do it now." What can we do today to make a difference if we want to change the world?

"So, if you want to change the world, don't back down from the sharks," McRaven said, meaning take an issue head-on. I reflect on my parent's encouragement when I was in college, struggling at Georgia Tech. I was the only female in most of my classes in Electrical Engineering. My dad always said, "Boys and girls are not equal; girls are better." This came from the parents of five girls. What they were saying was not to back down. Girls can do math and science just as well as boys. Keep working hard, and know you are just as capable as the opposite sex, even more so in some ways.

The speech says, "Be your very best in the darkest moment." When I think of some of my darkest moments, it was when my parents died—first my dad, then my mom. When my dad passed, my mom displayed the fortitude you needed when going through the "sickness" part of her wedding vows. She was there by his side, day in and day out. She was even dancing together at the hospital shortly before his death. Then, once the inevitable came, she mourned but didn't despair. She moved on to live her best life. She missed him terribly, but she became her best in the darkest moment, a good lesson for her children and grandchildren.

"Start singing when you're up to your neck in mud," McRaven explained about his final week of SEAL training. I know this was my mom's key to success. She was always an optimist. "You have a choice; you can have a good day or a bad day; choose a good day every day." I never heard my mom get angry, which seems impossible with a house of five daughters. She endured a lot of hardships in life. She survived the Great Depression, the loss of a child as well as the loss of her parents and husband. But she chose happiness and lived life to the fullest.

After McRaven's speech, he said, "If you want to change the world, don't ever, ever ring the bell." In the SEALs, if you want to stop the grueling training, you must ring the bell, and the misery will cease. Giving up is the easy out. That was also a lesson from my parents. Quitting is not an option. There may be a pivot, a change, or a redirection, but not quitting. Back in college, when I was frustrated with Electrical Engineering, dropping out was not an option. Instead, my parents encouraged me to change majors and to continue at Georgia Tech. Was it easy? No. Was it worth it? Yes. At that time, my graduation from college was my greatest accomplishment, mostly because I never rang that bell.

The commencement speech from 2014 was very inspiring to me. However, reflecting on my parents' lessons, I was raised with the same messages as the speech. No, I didn't undergo SEAL preparation or anything close to challenging training. From step one, Make Your Bed, through step 10, Never Ring the Bell, they taught me, "The world is Yours, and you can experience it and change it."

As we consider the power of small, consistent actions, it's interesting to reflect on how seemingly ordinary objects can also have a profound impact on our role across generations. One such example is the iconic Barbie doll, which has evolved significantly over the decades. Examining Barbie through the eyes of grandparents reveals not just a toy but a cultural touchstone that has shaped and reflected societal values across multiple generations. Let's delve into how this beloved doll has left an indelible mark on families and culture as an example of Social Capital.

Barbie Through the Generations: A Grandparents' Perspective

Let's take a trip down memory lane to explore the iconic world of Barbie dolls. From when our children played with these dolls to now watching our grandchildren enjoy them, Barbie has been a cherished part of our family's history. Join us as we share our thoughts, memories, and observations about how Barbie has evolved through the generations.

Barbie was "Born" in 1959, and in the beginning, Barbie was a revelation—a beautiful, poised doll that introduced a whole new realm of imaginative play. I remember the days when me and my sister's faces would light up at the sight of a new Barbie doll. The simple charm of those early Barbies, with their elegant outfits and graceful demeanor, continues to hold a special place in our hearts. My mom would sew clothes for Barbie, Ken, and Skipper. I still have these outfits in my Barbie suitcase, which I have kept for all these years.

As time passed, we witnessed a significant shift in Barbie's image. Introducing diverse dolls with various skin tones, body types, and cultural backgrounds made us appreciate how Barbie was evolving to better represent the world around us. It's heartwarming to see our grandchildren playing with dolls that more closely mirror the beautiful diversity of humanity.

One of the most impactful transformations has been Barbie's shift towards portraying robust and independent career women. This shift empowered our daughters and granddaughters, showing them that they could be anything they aspired to be. Barbie became a source of inspiration and aspiration for doctors, engineers, and astronauts.

Witnessing the timeless nature of Barbie's play brings me the most joy. Seeing our grandchildren playing with the same enthusiasm and creativity as our children did reminds me that some things remain constant across generations. From fashion shows to storytelling sessions, Barbie has been a bridge connecting us through shared play and cherished memories.

As grandparents, we're grateful for Barbie's enduring presence in our lives. From the classic era to the modern age, Barbie's evolution mirrors the changes in our society while maintaining her essence of imagination and play. Through Barbie, we've witnessed generations of children exploring their creativity, learning life lessons, and sharing countless moments of joy.

We look forward to seeing how Barbie continues to evolve and inspire the generations to come.

Reflecting on the evolution of Barbie through the generations offers a fascinating glimpse into how cultural values and family dynamics have shifted over time. Just as toys like Barbie provide insight into Social Capital so do personal experiences shared across different family settings. One such setting is the family-owned business, where teens often gain early work experience and life lessons. Transitioning from the world of iconic dolls to the everyday reality of a teen's journey behind the counter at the family liquor store, we uncover stories that reveal the complexities of adolescence, responsibility, and the unique challenges and rewards of contributing to a family enterprise leading to uncompromised family bonds. Let's explore these narratives and the valuable perspectives they offer.

A Teen's Journey Behind the Counter: Tales from the Family Liquor Store

In the heart of our small town stood a time-honored establishment with a story as rich as the spirits lining its shelves which instilled the Social Capital of family bonds. The family liquor store, once an ice cream parlor in the roaring twenties, transitioned through the years into a thriving hub for libations. My journey within its walls began at the tender age of 14, beginning a unique chapter that taught me the value of hard work, family bonds, and resilience.

Origins of the Family Business: Originating from the vision of my great-grandmother and her children, the family liquor store had modest beginnings. In 1908, Ratajack's embarked on its journey as a confectionery store, offering newspapers, magazines, tobacco, candy, and ice cream products, complemented by a pool room at the rear. Evolving with the times, the establishment underwent a series of transformations – first as a bar and dry goods store and eventually carving out its unique identity as a liquor store. The store's evolution is a testament to adaptability and entrepreneurial vigor, navigating through the challenges posed by economic downturns and shifts in societal trends.

Early Beginnings and Hard Work: My initiation into commerce came when I was just 14. With the family tradition deeply embedded in my roots, I began working alongside relatives, learning the ropes of customer service, inventory management, and the delicate art of recommending the perfect bottle for every occasion. The store, staffed exclusively by family members, became a melting pot of stories, laughter, and shared responsibilities.

Balancing High School and a Liquor Store: As my high school years unfolded, the collision of adolescence and the family business responsibilities became increasingly apparent. Juggling homework, extracurricular activities, and weekend shifts at the liquor store became my routine. The confluence of youthful innocence and the mature world of spirits provided a unique perspective on life. Little did I know that the challenges I faced in those early years would pale compared to a pivotal moment that tested my resolve and the store's legacy. Remarkably, 50 years ago last month, I received my first W-2 even though I started working at the store when I was five years old.

Facing Adversity: A Holdup at Gunpoint: One fateful evening, as I operated the counter during a quiet night, the serenity was shattered by an unexpected intruder. My hand trembled as I gave the cash from the cash register to the gunman, but I found it in me to press the alarm. The seconds felt like an eternity as I navigated the delicate dance of compliance and fear. It was a stark reminder that even within the familiar walls of family, adversity could strike unexpectedly. This incident, however, only strengthened my determination to safeguard the store and its legacy.

The End of an Era: As the late 1970s approached, the family liquor store faced a crossroads. Economic changes and personal considerations led to the bittersweet decision to sell the establishment. The end of an era brought mixed emotions – a sense of loss for a cherished family business and a recognition of the enduring lessons it bestowed upon us.

Working at the family liquor store from a young age was more than just a job; it was a journey that shaped my work ethic, resilience, and appreciation for family bonds. Every chapter contributed to the rich tapestry of my life, from its humble beginnings as an ice cream parlor to the challenges I faced during high school and the unexpected event of a holdup at gunpoint. As the store changed hands in 1978, the memories and lessons learned endured, leaving an indelible mark on the person I became. The family liquor store was not just a place of commerce; it was a living testament to the strength found in hard work, familial ties, and the unwavering spirit to adapt and endure.

Working behind the counter at a family liquor store presents teens with a unique family bonding experience by offering a perspective on responsibility, customer interaction, and the value of hard work. These experiences often shape their understanding of respect in the context of family and the wider community. Reflecting on tales of adolescence and business naturally leads us to a broader discussion on the importance of manners and kindness. The foundation of Social Capital is based on experiences that influence one's approach to interpersonal relationships and respect for others. Upholding respect and compassion in daily interactions enhances personal connections and fosters a more considerate and compassionate society. Let's explore how practicing these virtues can profoundly impact our lives and world.

R-E-S-P-E-C-T: Thoughts on Manners and Kindness

A long time ago, in a galaxy far, far away...I moved to Georgia to be a teacher. I was accustomed to answering questions with yes/no at my home galaxy of Illinois. To my surprise, in this galaxy known as the South, all my students would say "Yes, Ma'am" and "No, Ma'am." But after a little cultural immersion, I began appreciating this etiquette. I, too, began to use "Yes, Ma'am" and "No, Ma'am" and "Yes Sir" and "No Sir" when talking to others. I also had to get accustomed to being called "Miss Rosemarie." It doesn't matter if you are 10 or 110. In this galaxy, you will be called your name with a Miss (or Mr— my husband is regularly called Mr. John) in front of it. These are delightful signs of respect.

Now, realize I am not advocating for everyone to adopt a different galaxy's approach to manners. Still, it got me thinking about what we teach our grandchildren about respecting others. Here are some of my thoughts:

1. Dealing with others in person: Teach your children to be polite to everyone regardless of who they are or what they do. People are doing their jobs. I worked as a waitress while I was going to school. It was at an Officers Club on a Naval Base. One evening, I was serving a group of officers, including an Admiral who was wearing his dress whites. I was serving red wine from a rather heavy pitcher. I said, "Sir, would you like some wine?" The full pitcher was at my side, and I quickly brought it up, ready to pour. The pitcher hit the side of the table, and all contents sloshed out, covering the Admiral from head to chest. The Admiral put his fork down, red wine dripping from his nose, and said, "Thank you, miss, but I don't think I would like some right now." Self-restraint and politeness when things go south, especially accidental ones, are better than causing a scene. BTW, I was not fired, nor did the

Admiral require me to pay the dry-cleaning bill for his uniform.

2. It's the little things: Someone opens the door for you? Respond with a thank you. The maid at the motel gives me an extra towel. Thank you. The cashier hands you a receipt. Thank you. Thank you goes a long way and can be used liberally in any situation. "Would you like cream with your coffee?" "Yes, please."

3. Sitting etiquette: As children, we were taught to give up our seats, be in a doctor's office, bus, train, or any public space where seating was full. We were taught to give up our seats to someone who was elderly, disabled, mothers with babies in arms, or infirm. During my lifetime, I have done this many times. Doing something nice for someone you don't know is very self-satisfying. "Sir, please take my seat."

4. On the phone: I hate the "Press 1 for...." But that is part of life now. I never had to deal with this when I was a child. We had a party line and were polite to let whoever was on the line finish their conversation before we called someone— never had to 'dial 1' until I was an adult. This is

an excellent opportunity to teach your grandkids about patience and dealing with customer service. It would help if you reminded them they are real people trying to do their job. No matter how frustrated you are, it would help if you taught your grandchildren that being disrespectful should not be on the table.

5. Online: It is so easy to bully people online today, especially if you use an online nom-de-plume. Our grandchildren are using technology that did not exist when we were growing up, but it needs to be considered when teaching them respect for others. Teach your grandchildren to be polite online, regardless of the social media they are using. Being civil and levelheaded in using this media translates to their interaction with people in the four categories above.

Children are naturally self-centered and must be taught to respect others across all media, in-person and online. As grandparents, we can be the third-party provider of etiquette education regarding interacting with others. It is a unique opportunity as we spend time with our grandchildren. There are galaxies of things we can teach them. And you don't have to take them far, far, away.

Practicing respect and kindness in our daily interactions strengthens personal connections and lays the groundwork for more meaningful relationships. These values are crucial in maintaining bonds with loved ones living far away. Considering the impact of good manners and compassion, we focus on long-distance grandparenting's unique challenges and opportunities. Despite the physical distance, our Social Capital continues to develop. Grandparents can play a vital role in their grandchildren's lives, fostering solid and loving connections through thoughtful communication and creative engagement. Let's explore strategies for making the most of long-distance grandparenting and ensuring that these cherished relationships thrive across the miles.

Across the Miles: Making the Most of Your Long-Distance Grandparenting Role

Being a grandparent is a rewarding and cherished role. It's a chance to build strong connections with your grandchildren, watch them grow, and offer unconditional love and support. At least that's what "they" say.

However, "they" don't tell you how to accomplish that when distance separates you. Being a long-distance grandma, building a solid connection, watching them grow, and just "being there" can be challenging. How can you be a part of their daily lives, be there for the special moments, and develop a connection when you are miles away?

When my first grandchild was born, and he was just a little bundle drooling and pooping, being far away from him didn't seem like a big issue. Then, his world was tiny, and his understanding was limited to his immediate caregivers - his mom, dad, and Gigi, his mom's mom. He was focused only on his basic needs.

Now approaching his fourth birthday, my grandkid has developed a sense of self with opinions, an understanding of who to love, who provides comfort and support, and has identified who the family is from his perspective. I want to ensure he perceives me as a part of his family. However, how can I achieve this with the distance between us?

I can either play the victim or act, and this blog is about taking action. I've learned that regular communication is crucial.

Here are a few ideas on navigating the delicate balance between being part of their lives and intruding on the family.

1. Video Calls: Video calling platforms like Zoom or FaceTime are a great way to stay in touch with

your grandkids, even if you're far away. It's best to choose a specific time to establish a routine and make it a regular part of their life. During the video call, you can see each other, chat, and catch up on what's been happening in both of your lives. Instead of just making a phone call, it's better to use video calling as you can also see what they are wearing, eating, playing with, or even looking around the room for something to discuss. You can easily set up a Zoom call for free, and if you have an iPhone, you can use FaceTime, which is already a function on your phone. If you need help using these platforms, your kids can quickly help you.

My time is three hours earlier, which is breakfast time in Seattle. He is usually well-rested. During this time, his mother can take a few minutes while he and I discuss the upcoming day and recap the previous day.

2. Snail Mail: Since we live in the digital age, receiving physical letters or packages, particularly for children, can be thrilling. Taking some time to send your grandchild handwritten letters, postcards, or small surprise packages

can go a long way in strengthening your relationship with them. You could send them a drawing you made, a book you think they would enjoy, or even a package filled with their favorite treats. These tangible items will remind them of your presence in their life and show them that you care and think about them.

My grandson enjoys hearing jokes. If you want some, follow us on Facebook for "Silly Saturday," where we post a joke of the day. It is delightful to see how much he enjoys receiving them in his mailbox. Although he is only three and a half years old and his parents must read them for him, I know he will eventually be able to read them to me.

3. Create Shared Activities: Distance shouldn't limit your experiences with loved ones. Consider planning activities that you can do together virtually. For instance, you could both start reading the same book or choose a movie to watch at the same time while video chatting. Once you're done, you can discuss the story or film. This will help create shared memories and

provide an opportunity to bond despite the distance.

He currently loves Winnie the Pooh, so I get a list of his allowed movies. Since T.V. viewing is limited and his favorite shows are watched repeatedly, I can watch the film and have a chance to talk about it.

4. Virtual Storytime: Consider setting up a recurring virtual Storytime session where you can read books to your grandchildren. You can ask them to select a book they would like to read together, or you can surprise them with new stories. Use different voices to bring the characters to life and involve them in storytelling. This activity will help enhance their literary skills and strengthen the emotional bond between you and your grandchild.

Our "The Marshmallow Mystery" has been in his life since his birth; however, based on his age, what we "read" and "found" changed as his interest and age changed.

5. Celebrate Important Events: Try to be present for important events in your grandchild's life,

even if you can't physically be there. Use video calls to celebrate birthdays, graduations, holidays, or other special occasions. You can even prepare a special surprise for them, like ordering a cake or sending a personalized message they can open during the video call.

On Valentine's Day, we had a virtual cookie-making event over Zoom. It was a fun activity that we did together. While mixing the ingredients, we talked about everything and nothing, including the history of Valentine's Day, Valentine's activities we used to do at school, and even what our parents were planning to do for Valentine's Day.

6. Learn about their Interests: Show genuine interest in your grandchild's hobbies and activities. Ask them about their favorite sports, music, or hobbies, and take the time to learn more about them. Stay updated by following their social media accounts or subscribing to channels they enjoy. This will provide you with conversation topics and help you connect with them more personally.

The two interests we are currently discussing are soccer and swimming. He shares his likes and dislikes about each, which change weekly.

7. Plan Visits: Although being a long-distance grandma can be challenging, plan visits as often as possible. Try to be physically present during important milestones or contribute to special events. These visits will allow you to spend quality time with your grandchild, creating memories that will last a lifetime.

I decided to schedule a trip for my grandson's birthday and Christmas. However, since one of his grandmothers lives in town, I also wanted to spend some alone time with him and his parents. My goal, which is still in the planning stage, is for the four of us to travel somewhere together and share a unique experience. Not that the other grandmother and grandfather don't matter, but they already have daily activities.

Being a long-distance grandparent certainly comes with challenges. Still, with the right strategies and creativity, building and maintaining a solid and loving relationship with your grandchildren is possible, no matter the distance. Fostering our Social Capital asset is essential no matter the challenge.

Social Capital Conclusion

Social Capital is an important asset that consists of connections, networks, and beliefs that bring individuals together within a family, community, and society. It includes shared values, norms, and understandings that help people work together towards common goals. Social Capital strengthens relationships, influences our interactions, and expands our impact within our immediate circles and beyond. As families grow and extend their impact into the community, they enhance individual well-being and contribute to broader societal influence. Now, let's explore the specific bonds that unite a family's values, their Spiritual Capital.

Social Capital
Bingo

Social Capital is the act of fostering connections and relationships within our family and community by showing kindness to others. Check off the squares as your grandkid engages in these activities. The ultimate prize is discovering the joys of social engagement in a lively and interactive setting!

How can you help the community?	Visit a relative you don't normally see	Volunteer	Share something from your heritage with your friends	Join a face-to-face club
How do you solve differences with your friends?	How would you show school spirit this year	Draw a picture of your community	What is your favorite local business?	Help someone in need
Play with someone new	Share a toy	CJ CORKI	Hold the door open for some else	What is your favorite community event?
What do you want to be when you grow up?	List 5 qualities that make a good friend	Set the table	Take out the garbage	Have a neighborhood scavenger hunt
Participate in a community bike parade	Call all your grandparents to say hi	How can the neighborhood be improved?	Go to one festival this year	Say please & thank you 10 times in one day

SOCIAL CAPITAL ACTIVITY

Goals

How would you foster family relationships, community involvement, and friendships in your grandchildren?

Books:

- Kindness Makes Me Stronger by Elizabeth Cole

- Clifford's Good Deeds by Norman Bridwell

- See You Later, Alligator by Sally Hopgood

- Name Your Favorite: _____

Questions to Ask:

- What community activities would you like to be involved in?
- What random acts of kindness would you like to do?
- What family activities do you think we can do together that would be fun and also help us build stronger relationships and connect with our community?

Chapter 5

Spiritual Capital: The Role of Values in Enriching Lives

Trust is the highest form of human motivation. It brings out the very best in people. But it takes time and patience, and it doesn't preclude the necessity to train and develop people so that their competency can rise to the level of that trust. Stephen R. Covey

Spiritual Capital Introduction

Spiritual Capital represents the intangible resources within individuals and families that derive from their spiritual beliefs, values, and practices. It encompasses aspects such as faith, generosity, compassion, character, and a sense of purpose or transcendence. It encompasses the inner resources that guide individuals and families toward fulfillment, resilience, and a deeper connection to each other and the world around them. In an era marked by rapid change and uncertainty, understanding and nurturing Spiritual Capital offers a pathway toward holistic well-being, a meaningful life, and a sense of purpose.

In contrast to the lofty ideals of Spiritual Capital, sometimes simple, everyday acts of integrity captivate our attention and highlight the more whimsical aspects of being raised in a family with faith.

Penniless Pretzel Pilfering: The Art of Snagging a Snack

Picture this: It's a sunny September school day in a quaint little town where everyone knows your family inside and out, including your family's bustling business. It's snack Tuesday, and like clockwork, the solemn nuns take the scheduled 10-minute snack break where the opportunity to purchase a penny candy or a single-stick salted pretzel on the honor system has just begun. The line was about to be open for their hungry guests.

The 6-year-olds knew the drill. The items were pulled from their dark hiding place and placed on the front schoolroom desks. The long-awaited permission to come forward resulted in the jarring sound of chairs scraping on the floor and the rushing to get ahead of one another as if there were only a handful of goodies for buying. We were sternly ushered into a single file line, the feeling of warm pennies in their hands as they were counted and re-counted as we wobbled to the front of the line. Imagine you're a young bundle of sunshine, standing in that line with a growling tummy and not even a penny in her pocket. This was the first of many life conflicts that this young 6-year-old had to face.

Yes, this bundle of sunshine was me. The pretzels were usually delivered to the school in a large square box, and as the days turned into weeks, the freshness of the pretzels dropped significantly. Even at age 6, we quickly learned that when a new box was brought out and the tape cut open, that was the day that beckons you with the allure of that perfectly golden and salted treat and that's when my dilemma unfolded. No pennies. Steal or not to steal. What were the pros? No one would know. After all, it was an honor system. What was the con? I would know.

Yes, it's a classic moral tug-of-war, where the battle between my rumbling stomach and my inner youthful hero takes center stage. Buckle up because we're about to dive into the world of tough decisions and life lessons in the most unexpected places.

As a child, I learned in Catholic school that stealing was wrong. As a family member in the business, trust, honesty, and looking out for "stealers" was part of our job as we "worked" the store. The rules were clear: You do not steal, period.

In our everyday lives, we encounter numerous ethical dilemmas, some seemingly trivial but thought-provoking. We all have them; remember that our kids and grandkids have them too. So, let's use them. Yes, the good, the bad, and the ugly. Our lifetime of experiences, knowing what we know, and the tough decisions we made to do "the right thing" or sharing the consequences of making the wrong one is one way to help the next generation deal with those predicaments they might be struggling with. Honest sharing of our impulses and desires is a priceless conversation. After all, our power comes from sharing that none of us are perfect. Remember, these conversations should not be punitive but rather an opportunity to talk about the values we uphold and our responsibility towards society and family.

So, what was that 6-year-old child's decision to steal or not steal that lone pretzel? I took that pretzel and turned. Before I could take five steps back towards my seat, I recognized the wrongness of stealing and, with a six-year-old moral code, turned around, handed it back to the nun, and said I didn't have a penny to pay for it. Sorry.

That sober-looking nun didn't miss a beat and handed it back to me and said, bring a penny back tomorrow. It's good because I have already taken a bite out of it!

Thank you, mom, dad, and grandma. By fostering a solid moral foundation, I was grounded in values that promote fairness, compassion, and honesty. Let's pay that forward. So, consider your moral values and how you will pass them on to future generations.

I Like Bike: Changing the Paradigm of Giving

Paying it forward. How do you give back? It isn't just about money. Although it takes money to buy things to give back, it makes a more significant impact by giving a physical item rather than just cash. There are seven ways to live generously: Thoughts, Words, Influence, Time, Attention, Belonging, and Money. How can you incorporate giving into everyday living? Start by sharing the stories, "I like _____."

An Immigrant Family was Robbed! It didn't make the headlines, but it was a severe blow to this family since they lost their bike used for transportation to work. After reading their story in the newspaper, some good Samaritans decided to make a difference. Although they were strangers, this young family purchased new bikes to give to them. The head of the immigrant household did not speak English, but when his son translated that the bike was for him, he repeatedly said with a grin, I like bike, I like bike. Not asking for anything in return, the givers felt a "helper high" from the experience. However, the real lesson is the shift in thinking about giving back.

Thoughts: Many times, we think the worst of people. If someone shows up late and is inconsiderate of other people's time, they may show passive-aggressive behavior. Or we think they are lazy, unorganized, or even rude. However, having the generosity of thoughts gives that person the benefit of the doubt. They might have run into traffic. They could have dealt with screaming children or a dog that wouldn't listen to come inside. I hate being late, and I was a repeat offender of tardiness when my kids were in elementary school. Yes, I was that late parent who rushed into the after-school care to pick up my kids after hours. However, the teachers showed empathy to this stressed-out working mom. I wasn't judged; I was given the gift of compassion. Give the gift of encouraging thoughts to parents.

Words: Sticks and stones may break my bones, but words can never hurt me, which is a false narrative. Words mean something. People, especially children, notice when you criticize, demoralize, or even make a filipin passing remark. Early in my kid's life, I would remark on my kid's lack of basketball ability. Not because they played but because they were the shortest in their class. It was never directed to them but to fellow parents. Never in my wildest dreams did I think they overheard me. Of course, they never played basketball for that reason. They would pick up a basketball to play if they only heard love and support, even from the sidelines. Give the gift of positive words to children.

Influence: Whom do you know? Help people with your network. Do the children need a tutor, a dance teacher, or a trainer? The busy mom may need a free day by using a babysitter, house cleaner, or driver. If you know someone who can help, recommendations are essential. I remember when we moved to Michigan, looking for a pediatric doctor. I would ask anyone with kids whom they recommend. Don't take this namedrop lightly. It is truly a part of being generous.

Time: Who has extra time? The answer is nobody. The gift of time is one of the most coveted. Most people will value the contribution of time over money. Visiting grandparents in the nursing home might not be the most favorite thing for grandchildren, but it will be the most remembered. If done right, it will be a win-win for the grandchild, parent, and grandparent. I remember visiting my grandmother in a nursing home in high school. It wasn't enjoyable. The place smelled of urine, and the atmosphere was depressing. It's not a teenager thing. But reflecting on those times, the visits brought joy to my mom and grandmother. The gift of time is priceless.

Attention: If you cannot be anything else, be present. Today, everyone has their head down on their cell phones. It is a distraction from the day-to-day enjoyment of life. Who they are with, where they are visiting, and what they eat are typical posts on social media. What about the person next to you, especially the young children? Don't they deserve the attention of a parent or grandparent? Children regularly ask to "look at me." Make sure you do. If you don't, you could miss their big moment with their first steps, first words, or first sporting event score. Be giving of your attention.

Belongings: You might think it is just stuff, but someone's junk is someone else's treasure. Recently, we had a guest stay at our historic property, Belle-Hampton. She spent the summers here growing up. She reminisced about the beautiful family dinners with blue and white China in the dining room. She secretly thought about snatching a plate as a remembrance. After several discussions, I asked her if she would like one as a souvenir. She cried. The meaningfulness of having an item from her childhood was touching. A simple gift of belongings can make a difference.

Money: Yes, a financial contribution is still significant. It keeps the lights on. We were on the

Kearney Area Children's Museum board when we lived in Nebraska. My husband was the treasurer. They were so poorly run that the electric company was scheduled to turn off the lights. Paying your bills was the answer. However, the museum's finances were operating in the negative. We spent it forward and paid the bill. For us to get income, we needed lights. Although there are many ways to contribute, sometimes money is the only answer.

How can you cultivate generosity in your everyday life? Think about ways to pay it forward using these buckets of ways to give back. What can you do today that will make a difference? Join the challenge. As a grandparent, ask your grandchild what is essential to them. Whatever their interest, the zoo or the environment, work with them to contribute in their name. Or create a generosity jar. Have them write down how someone they saw is being generous; note the giving category. Make the decision today to "I Like Giving." Be the difference.

But sometimes, our beliefs and traditions demonstrate our generosity within the family. Holidays such as Christmas are the giving season for Spiritual Capital.

Faith Woven in Tradition: A Holiday Journey of Resilience and Blessings

Our family's religious beliefs and unique traditions are a big part of who we are and how we see the world. I am betting that this is no different from you.

We were raised Catholic and have continued that belief into adulthood. It helps us navigate our day-to-day routine and those extra special occasions.

So, here's a secret I wanted to share. We recently sold our house, and I must tell you that the whole story of selling our house to build our forever home is like a mash-up of faith, hope, and practicality. You won't believe it, but we have this tradition where we bury a St. Joseph statue in our house's front yard. There are specific rules, such as it must be upside down and facing the house. We have done it for every house sale, which helps get the property sold faster. Crazy, right? But it's like showing that we trust in some higher power and believe in its symbolism. And believe it or not, we put our house on the market, and poof! Sold on the very first day! It felt like a total miracle. It made us even more sure that prayers and traditions pack a punch.

So, this quick sale was a double-edged sword - we hit this major snag on closing our new place, which meant we needed a place to live for a solid month. Can you believe that played havoc on our holiday plans, too? But guess what? We didn't let it get us down. Well, if truth be told, we were a little concerned, but our family stayed strong and made it a point to celebrate Christmas as one unit. Luckily, or as fate would have it, our friends were kind enough to lend us their townhouse, where we had to switch up our usual traditions. We jerry-rigged a tiny fake tree and threw up some stockings, entering the Christmas spirit. It shows that we can roll with the punches and keep the holiday magic alive no matter what crazy curveballs life throws.

Of course, going to church was part of our ritual, and we attempted to give ourselves enough time to attend a mega Christmas Eve mass that was jam-packed with people. Finding a seat was a struggle, but we stayed patient and grateful. The mass was the perfect blend of regular attendees alongside those who only show up for Christmas and Easter. It showed how our community can come together to celebrate the holiness of the season. And it wasn't just the religious stuff that brought us closer -- as we made our way back home, we checked on that mouthwatering Back Creek Wagyu roast we had in the oven for our Christmas Eve dinner. Later, we decided to spice things up and play games like Farkle and Rummikub. It might not have been the typical setting, but we had such a blast and created memories that will stay with all of us for a long time.

Christmas morning was fantastic! We had so much fun tearing into presents, munching on delicious cinnamon rolls, and sipping yummy

Mimosas. It was a spur-of-the-moment celebration that reminded us how important family is and showed us that we can find happiness no matter what life throws our way.

During our holiday celebrations, we took time to think about all the Christmas traditions we incorporated into our lives. Oplatki is a Polish tradition of sharing wafers and wishing the recipient joy. This tradition started in early Christian times, and these white wafers are made from flour and water. They're remarkably delicate and have Christmas pictures etched into them, like the Nativity scene. Even though we didn't have any Oplatki this year, since they were packed somewhere in our storage unit, we did pass on individual Christmas wishes, and it didn't take away from how fantastic our Christmas was. We believe in the love and support of friendship and family, which makes Christmas wonderful and unique. Even though we did things differently this year, the joy of being together and creating memories reminded us of what Christmas is all about.

We're excited for our new place in Florida to be all set, but as our homelessness continues, we decided to join family in Atlanta. We will spend time with our two daughters and some awesome sisters. Since it was New Year's, we couldn't pass up the chance of devouring black-eyed peas and collard greens, a Southern tradition.

To make things even better, an employee offered us a spot in an empty apartment while we were there. It showed us how tightly we're all connected. The fun didn't stop there, though. We ended up going on a last-minute cruise that was all about hockey. Talk about the unexpected! It shone a light on our faith-filled journey's exciting and adventurous nature.

In the tapestry of our beliefs and traditions, the awesome stuff that makes up our lives, we find this fantastic thread of resilience, adaptability, and gratitude. It's this and faith that holds everything together. Our faith in God and the extraordinary group of family and friends keep us going strong, even when things get crazy. No matter how chaotic life gets, our religion serves as a flashlight, reminding us that we're blessed with love from our family and the grace of our faith. What would you do in a homeless situation?

Nurturing Spiritual Capital: A Gift for Future Generations

Teaching your grandchildren about Spiritual Capital is a profoundly meaningful and enduring gift that can impact their character and values throughout their lives. Instilling these profound principles can take various forms, and each aspect is essential in nurturing their spiritual growth.

First and foremost, leading by example is the cornerstone of this journey. When you embody virtues like honesty, kindness, empathy, and humility in everyday life, your actions and behaviors serve as a powerful model for your grandchildren. They will not only witness these virtues in action but also gain insights into the importance of these qualities. Sharing personal stories that highlight how these principles have guided your decisions and shaped your character reinforces the significance of these values. Your stories become a repository of wisdom, and your grandchildren will come to understand that these principles are not mere words but lived experiences. This emphasis on leading by example empowers you to make a significant impact on your grandchildren's spiritual growth.

Creating an open door to dialogue is equally critical. By engaging your grandchildren in meaningful conversations about spirituality and values, you encourage them to ask questions, express their thoughts, and share their experiences. This fosters a deep sense of trust and security, enabling them to freely discuss their beliefs and concerns. These dialogues provide a platform for them to explore their own spiritual journey, allowing them to develop a deeper connection with their beliefs and values. This sense of security and trust can reassure you that you are creating a safe space for your grandchildren to grow spiritually.

Furthermore, sharing your accumulated wisdom is a vital component of this educational process.

Your life experiences have provided you with a treasure trove of insights. When you recount the challenges you've faced and how your spiritual beliefs guided you through them, you offer invaluable life lessons. Your personal anecdotes serve as powerful tools for teaching Spiritual Capital, illustrating the practical application of these beliefs in navigating life's ups and downs. The joy and fulfillment that come from sharing these experiences can be a source of great motivation for you and a powerful inspiration for your grandchildren.

Encouraging exploration and openness to diverse spiritual and philosophical traditions is another essential facet of this journey. Exposing your grandchildren to various belief systems, from different religions to secular philosophies, empowers them to develop a broader perspective. This exposure enriches their understanding of other cultures and perspectives and allows them to find what resonates with them spiritually. Please encourage them to ask questions, seek knowledge, and ultimately form their beliefs.

In addition to intellectual exploration, instilling mindfulness and gratitude in your grandchildren is a powerful practice. By teaching them to appreciate the beauty of the present moment and to be thankful for the blessings in their lives, you provide them with tools for introspection and self-awareness. Activities like meditation or nature walks can help them connect with their inner selves and the world, fostering a more profound sense of spirituality.

Finally, engaging in acts of service together is a practical way to instill the importance of giving back and nurturing empathy and compassion. Volunteering as a family teaches the value of helping others and allows your grandchildren to experience the joy that comes from being a positive force in the community. These shared experiences can have a profound impact on their understanding of humanity's interconnectedness and the role of compassion in our spiritual journey.

This multi-faceted approach ensures you pass on a rich and comprehensive spiritual legacy to your grandchildren, equipping them with the tools and values they need to navigate life with purpose, resilience, and a solid moral compass. This gift is not just for the present but will continue to enrich their lives and the lives of generations to come, making it a cherished inheritance that transcends time.

However, it is essential to understand that Spiritual Capital is NOT About Going to Church. While religious institutions can play a role, Spiritual Capital encompasses a broader range of beliefs, values, and practices that transcend traditional religious activities.

Spiritual Capital is NOT About Going to Church

Do you go to church? This is not a judgment question, just a simple question. Any church, synagogue, mosque, or temple in the past seven days? If you have, you are one of the 34% of the US adult population that regularly attend a religious service.

I was part of that statistic as a kid. I was raised Roman Catholic, more specifically, Polish Roman Catholic. Learning the hymns, memorizing the prayers, studying the procedures of genuflection, the saints, the sign of the cross, and everything in between was how, back in my day, we developed our Spiritual Capital.

Regardless of what we think about teaching any specific religion, in today's rapidly changing and increasingly global society, the concept of Spiritual Capital has expanded beyond its traditional understanding. While Financial and Human Capital significantly contribute to personal and societal success, an emerging and equally important type of capital has gained attention: Spiritual Capital. Despite differing opinions on teaching specific religions, it is essential to recognize the value of Spiritual Capital in our changing world.

Spiritual Capital covers the qualities and resources that enhance our sense of purpose, meaning, and fulfillment in life. It goes beyond the religious beliefs and practices I observed as a kid. It encompasses a broader range of experiences that deepen our connection with ourselves, others, and the world around us. This insight can include a sense of awe and wonder when taking a moment to observe the wonders of nature. It's also all about knowing what's important to us, working on being better, and being kind and understanding to others.

One of the reasons I enjoyed going to church was not the rituals of the service, not the gospel, and not even the Hallelujah choir. What I enjoyed most was that this was the only 45 minutes that belonged to me, where I could sit quietly with no devices or distractions and think. Yep, think. It might be about a problem I need to solve, an internal conundrum, or even a chance to take time to think about the past and future.

Now, as an adult with a grandchild, I feel that I have the responsibility to help him find his special place to think about decisions to be made, some ethical debates that he might be facing, and to allow him to empower himself to lead a meaningful life. His family does not lack any financial resources, so I also want to help him find a way to contribute positively to his community.

He's a smart kid, and my job is to help him tap into his inner strength and exercise the values he is being taught. Everyone's life is a series of ups and downs, and the gift I want to give him doesn't come in wrapping paper and a bow but rather the tools to navigate life's challenges with resilience and wisdom. If, in addition, he learns to recognize that his actions and choices have a ripple effect that extends beyond himself, I will be a happy grandma. We, grandparents, are in this together and have the power to reinforce and support this significant development.

So, I hope that after reading this, when you think about Spiritual Capital, you think beyond going to church and the religious contexts that are a part of any particular religious traditions. To me, it's more significant than that! It is what makes us human, enabling us to seek purpose and find meaning in life's often chaotic and unpredictable journey.

Let's help our grandkids learn the importance of slowing down, reflecting, and connecting with their inner selves and the world around them. Yes, we know their days are often prioritized with school, homework, and sports. How about teaching them to add prioritizing values such as compassion, kindness, and empathy? Adding these 3 points can transform not only their own lives but also the communities and societies we reside in. Consider what we will leave behind if we help our grandkids unlock their full potential and create a more compassionate and harmonious next generation.

Discovering Your Path: A Heartfelt Guide for Grandchildren

Smartphones, social media, video games, and TV are all distractions for even the littlest of kids today. Pressures from adults on issues such as climate change, sexual identity, and DEI affect youngsters' mental health. In a world full of uncertainty, many children find themselves lost, without guidance or direction. As grandparents, we are not just bystanders in this journey but active participants. We have the power to assist them in finding their path, influence their dreams, and guide them toward a sense of fulfillment. But how do you help them discover their dreams? Let's explore this journey of self-discovery and how to navigate it with your grandchildren.

Let's delve into the concept of 'purpose' and its profound significance. Life is an exhilarating adventure, and one of the most transformative quests they will embark on is discovering their dreams. Their dreams are not just whims but a compass that guides them towards a fulfilling and meaningful life, their purpose. These are not just big concepts but the keys to unlocking their potential, and we can help them understand and embrace them.

What is Purpose?

Your purpose is the reason you feel excited to wake up in the morning. It's what makes you feel alive and gives your life direction. It can be something you're passionate about, a talent you want to share with the world, or a cause you care deeply about.

When our youngest son was little, he was captivated by soccer. It was more than just a game to him; it was his passion, his joy, and his purpose. If he wasn't playing soccer, he was practicing soccer. If he wasn't practicing it, he was playing soccer video games or watching his favorite team, Manchester United. During his youth, he played for the regional team and traveled to Europe, where he visited his dream team's stadium. As he got older, he won state and national championships. Although he never dreamed of playing professionally, he achieved his goals, and that's what finding your purpose is all about.

Why Finding Your Purpose is Important

Discuss with your grandkids why finding your purpose is critical to their development.

Direction: Having a purpose helps you know where you want to go and what steps to take.

Motivation: It gives you a reason to keep going, even when things get tough.

Happiness: Doing things that matter to you brings joy and satisfaction.

Impact: Your purpose often involves helping others, which can improve the world.

Our son's soccer experience has shaped him as an adult. He learned teamwork, leadership, discipline, respect, fair play, and resilience. He experienced it the hard way, with fair play and resilience by an injury. He was targeted by the other team to be taken out of the game. And within a moment of an illegal tackle in the box, his soccer was over. As he waved to the fans from the ambulance, he waved goodbye to soccer.

Did the referees red-card the tackle? No, there was no call, just a referee waving to "play on." Was that fair? Well, life isn't fair; lesson learned. Instead, he showed resilience and recovered from a severe injury, not missing school work and graduating from college, leading to his next phase of life. He gathered his experiences with his first sense of purpose to move to the next level of life.

Soccer's impact on his life also impacted his teammates, by showing sportsmanship and respect. Living his dreams with integrity, passion, and love of the game made all the difference.

Steps to Discovering Your Purpose

Use the following exercise with your grandkids:

Reflect on What You Love: Consider what activities make you lose track of time. Do you love drawing, playing sports, reading, or helping others? These activities can give you clues about your purpose.

Try New Things: Don't be afraid to explore and experiment. Join clubs, try new hobbies or volunteer. Sometimes, you find your purpose by stepping out of your comfort zone.

Listen to Your Heart: Pay attention to what feels right to you. Your inner voice can guide you towards what truly matters to you.

Talk to Others: Share your thoughts with family, friends, and teachers. They can offer insights and see things about you that you might not notice.

Set Goals: Once you have an idea of your purpose, set small goals to move towards it. This can give you a sense of direction and achievement.

Stay Open-Minded: Remember, your purpose might change as you grow. Be open to new experiences and allow your purpose to evolve.

As a grandparent, you can ask these questions with your grandkids to help them brainstorm what might be important to them. Be patient; they might not know right away, and several dreams might unfold over time. Although our son discovered early on his dream of soccer, his next dream wasn't so clear.

Because sports, not just soccer, is his passion, it was natural for him to choose a major in Sports Management. Although his interest was there, once he got into the world of sports as a business, he knew it wasn't his purpose. After some challenging positions on the business side of soccer and football, he knew he had to pivot. Although his whole life was sports, returning to school for an MBA was his new goal. Because of an open mind and his family's support, he achieved his next stage in life.

Living Your Purpose

Talk about the following ideas with your grandkids on living their dreams:

Align Your Actions: Make sure your daily activities match your purpose. If you love helping others, find ways to volunteer or support friends.

Embrace Challenges: Don't be afraid of obstacles. They are opportunities to learn and grow stronger in your purpose.

Practice Gratitude: Be thankful for the progress you make. Celebrating small achievements can keep you motivated.

Connect with Supportive People: Surround yourself with people encouraging and inspiring you. They can help you stay on track.

Give Back: Part of finding your purpose is about making a difference. Look for ways to contribute to your community or support causes you care about.

One of our son's ways of giving back combined his love for soccer with his gratitude for his athleticism. He has always been passionate about helping special needs children. He has coached Top Soccer kids with Down syndrome since he was little. The experience of working with kids who didn't have an athletic gift but lived with joy and happiness in their hearts made an impact on his life; always be grateful.

Helping your grandchildren find their purpose is an exciting journey that can lead to a fulfilling and meaningful life. It's about helping them discover what makes them happy, use their unique talents, and make a positive impact on the world. Remember, their purpose doesn't have to be something big or grand—it just needs to be meaningful to them.

Spiritual Capital Conclusion

Spiritual Capital emerges as a profound yet often overlooked dimension of a family's assets, encompassing the richness of inner resources that contribute to individual and family flourishing. As your family grapples with complex challenges and uncertainties, recognizing the value of Spiritual Capital becomes increasingly pertinent. It serves as a guiding force, offering solace, strength, and a sense of purpose amidst adversity. Moreover, Spiritual Capital fosters empathy, compassion, and interconnectedness, laying the foundation for resilient communities and a more harmonious world. By nurturing and cultivating Spiritual Capital within us and our family, we can embark on a journey toward deeper fulfillment, meaningful relationships, and a greater sense of collective purpose.

Spiritual Capital
Bingo

This bingo is designed to support the development of children's core values. It includes their beliefs, practices, and how they seek meaning and purpose as they transition to adulthood. It helps you guide them in contemplating life's big questions. As your grandchild participates in these enriching experiences, mark off the squares.

Do Yoga	Where is your special place to go and think?	Perform an act of kindness	Make up a prayer	What does it mean to lie?
Express gratitude to someone	Go "forest bathing"	Read a book that inspires you	What does being "mindful" mean?	Show someone you love and care for them
What are you thankful for?	When was it hardest to tell the truth?	CJ CORKI	What do you hope for?	Spend 5 minutes alone with no distractions
Do something you think is generous	What was a time that you were patient?	Show empathy to mom or dad	Tell how you are thoughtful	Donate toys that you don't play with anymore
How do you find strength when things are hard?	What is important to you?	Read a book about someone who had to overcome something	Do a random act of kindness	Find a song that inspires you

SPRITUAL CAPITAL ACTIVITY

Goals

How do you plan to develop your grandchildren's core values and beliefs?

Books:

- My Magical Choices by Becky Cummings

- What Should Danny Do? by Adir Levy

- The Wonderful Things You Will Be by Emily Winfield Martin

- Name Your Favorite: _____

Questions to Ask:

- What activities do you think we could add to your daily or weekly routine that would help you develop a better understanding of values?
- What are some ways we can be generous as a family?
- What kind of family activities do you think would help us all feel more grateful and connected?

Chapter 6

Legacy Capital: Passing Down History, Harmony and Heritance

Create Your Legacy, and Pass the Baton.

Billie Jean King

Legacy Capital Introduction

In life's journey, one of the most profound legacies we can leave behind doesn't just lie in the wealth we gain, but in the impact and contributions we leave for future generations.
Legacy Capital is like a quilt connecting the past, present, and future of our family's identity and history. It's made up of special things we hold dear and the stories we share, creating wonderful memories for our family.

This forms the bedrock upon which future generations can build their success. It encompasses the rich tapestry of family stories and represents your role as a unifier rather than the central figure of the family. By intentionally sharing our experiences and lessons learned, we can positively shape our grandchildren's character, ambitions, and ability to navigate the complexities of the world. This section outlining practical strategies and heartfelt approaches to enrich our grandchildren's lives, ensuring they inherit more than just material wealth but a treasure trove of wisdom and strength to carry forward through their lives.

The following stories are intended to inspire you to reflect on your own experiences and think about how you can effectively pass on your traditions, insights, and history to your grandchildren.

Fading Footprints: Unraveling the Tapestry of Family History

We start this Legacy Capital journey by reflecting on the history of our family, the early experiences, and the influences that have shaped us into who we are today.

Embarking on a journey to uncover our past often reveals unexpected surprises waiting to be unearthed, offering new insights into who we are and where we come from. So, come with me as we unwrap the past.

Once upon a time, in the quaint hamlet of North Chicago, nestled between the Great Lakes Naval Training Center and the state line of Wisconsin, there lived five young girls. They were known for their strong work ethic, kind hearts, and insatiable curiosities. Their days were spent working in the family business based in the heart of the hamlet. The family business began in the early 1900s, and their great-grandmother purchased the land alone long before women's lib became a thing.

Where does your story begin?

I started this story with a simple but powerful piece of history, which I hope can inspire you to trace your family lineages and get excited about connecting with the past. Like you, I have always known my immediate family, but only as I got older did I realize there is much more about who I am based on knowing the past and how their decisions and genetic makeup affected me. Heavy, I know, and you may think this is too difficult to accomplish, but as "they" say, it only begins with one step. Look around your family right now. Is an aunt, a family friend, or a grandparent still around? They don't have to live close by, and you don't even have to have a strong relationship with them. Don't stop for a moment; reach out to them and find out what they remember.

Family stories are my favorite because they are seasoned with what happened during that era. Those stories are priceless. My mom told a story about my great-grandmother, who purchased commercial property independently and then told her husband what she accomplished and what her vision was after the purchase was complete. This was 1908.

If there may be no relatives or family friends, there are still numerous routes for getting information. Research using various records and sources like birth certificates, marriage licenses, census data, and other historical documents to construct a family tree. Ancestry.com and other similar sites can be a starting point.

The importance of learning about your past can vary, which is why I named this story about the Fading Footprints. If you don't take the step today, an opportunity might pass, and every day missed is another footprint fading. Each of us is different, as are our stories. Here are several reasons why I consider it valuable to share your past:

1- Think about your kids – what do you want them to know or remember? This single act of stepping back and thinking about what you want your kids to remember will help you start preserving family stories, traditions, and cultural heritage and passing them from one generation to another. What was done in the past? Tell them. What about you? What activities or traditions do you currently do? Tell them why.

Preserving history can go back decades but can also start with you and your current traditions. I have stories of my past, but with the addition of a spouse, he also had traditions and stories. Don't forget both sides of the family. The merging of traditions starts new traditions. My husband and his family used to always go to the Indiana Dunes. This was a fall ritual where his grandma and mom stopped their daily activities and went to the beach to gather sand and watch the sunset. The purpose was more significant than the sand or the sunset; they discussed their vision for the next year and how they did with the previous year's plan. This tradition moved from the dunes to Mission Bay in San Diego, but every year for 25 years, one day was dedicated to planning the following year. We incorporated that tradition into our lives, and it continues.

2—Identity and Belonging: Knowing one's family history provides a sense of identity and belonging. It can help each of us understand our heritage, cultural background, and ancestors' experiences.

3- Medical History: Genealogy can be priceless for understanding inherited health conditions and genetic traits within a family. Knowing ancestors' medical history can provide insights into potential health risks for current and future generations. My husband was adopted. His biological father was alive, but he had no contact with him. When we had our daughter, I knew my family's medical history, but my husband was missing his father's genetic makeup. He hired a private detective to find him, not because he wanted to build a relationship 40 years later, even though he did, but rather to find out "what he died from." That genetic piece didn't matter until he realized that knowledge was more important than just for him.

4- Researching Ancestors: Many people engage in genealogy to learn more about their ancestors, their lives, and the challenges they faced. Discovering the stories of one's ancestors can be a rewarding and enlightening experience.

I really hope this motivates you to realize how much power you have and pushes you to act right away. Just think, your family history can help you understand your own personal story and the stories of those you're connected to. If you start digging into your genealogy now and create a sense of connection between the past, present, and future, your kids and grandkids will be grateful to you.

Why not take this chance to begin your journey of figuring yourself out and building connections? Connect the dots between your past, present, and future. You can be the one who tells the story and leaves a lasting impact that will be remembered for years to come. As you navigate life's ups and downs, remember that your future family will cherish the choices you make today. Your legacy is waiting for you, and the admiration of future generations will be the ultimate payoff.

Let's talk about symbols that encompass traditions that might also round out the legacy.

Families Unite Through Family Emblems, Ancestral Banners, and Homestead Art

Family flags, emblems, and banners play a significant role in Legacy Capital by serving as powerful symbols and traditions that represent a family's history, values, and heritage. These symbols encapsulate the essence of a family's identity and the principles passed down through generations, reinforcing continuity and connection. By passing down these symbols, families actively engage in legacy building, ensuring their values, achievements, and heritage are remembered and cherished by future generations.

Have you ever thought about crafting a family symbol? Family symbols such as crests, flags, and barn quilts are not just artifacts but also timeless and living emblems of our shared lineage and heritage. They stand as guardians of our shared history and echo with the whispers of our ancestors' dreams and values. These symbols bind generations like a sturdy thread, weaving through the tapestry of time and igniting a flame of familial pride and unity. They light the way for our collective aspirations to shine through the ages.

Family Crest

A family crest is a unique and hereditary symbol or design representing a particular family or clan. It is often used as a part of a larger heraldic achievement, including a shield, motto, supporters, and other elements.

The Hoge family crest, belonging to my husband's lineage, has its roots in Scotland and dates to the early 1100s. "Dat Gloria Vires" is a Latin quote consistent with all the visual variations of the crest. It means "Strength in Name." This is a high standard to live up to, having a strong name not for decades but centuries. Along with its long history and legacy, it represents ethics, notoriety, achievement, and reputation.

It is worth noting that not every family has a family crest. Coats of arms were typically reserved for the wealthy, such as nobles, rich merchants, and administrators. If your ancestors were poor farmers, they would unlikely have a coat of arms. Therefore, you may not find one if you are searching for your family crest.

Anyone can adopt a coat of arms, and registration is not required. However, using someone else's coat of arms is unacceptable. Coats of arms were initially used to distinguish one family from another, and adopting a coat of arms that belongs to another family violates heraldic rules and is considered "usurpation."

The good news is that you can always create one of your own. Creating a family crest is more than choosing a few symbols and colors. It is a way to celebrate your family's history and accomplishments while preserving your legacy for future generations. But there are other ways to bring symbols into your family besides a crest.

Family Flags

The meaning and use of a family flag can differ significantly and may depend on the family's customs and inclinations. In my case, my sisters and I used it to indicate a particular occasion, whereas my family preferred to use it to mark milestones in a series of events.

During our final family vacation to Colorado and Wyoming in the 1960s, we decided to commemorate the occasion by creating a family flag. The flag featured a road runner, symbolizing our family's characteristics: quick thinking, resourcefulness, endurance, communication, and adaptability.

We aimed to go on a family climb in Estes Park, Colorado, a town in the Rocky Mountains. My sisters, who are all about ten years older than me, led the way. However, when we reached a steep incline, they decided to lift me up to achieve our goal together.

My parents had a different vision. Being only four years old, they called me back and didn't want me to make the dangerous incline. My sisters successfully planted the flag on the mountain to achieve our charge. It wasn't until forty years later that we recreated the climb, and I could join them on the mountaintop. This time in Wyoming. For this sister's weekend event, we dusted off our family flag. The mission was the same: go to the top of the mountain. Instead of making the dangerous climb, we decided to take the gondola. We took pictures to remember the trip, but we carefully folded the flag and brought it home to store for posterity.

Inspired by our Szostak family flag, our family, the Hoge's, decided to create one of our own, taking some aspects of the family crest. However, this flag didn't represent one event but rather a series of events. Each time we accomplished a significant goal, we would take a picture of ourselves with the flag to represent us "moving the flag" to become the person we want to be. Some of us even solicited signatures from people who journeyed with us.

Our son Peyton climbed Mt Rainer and Kilimanjaro, where he proudly displayed our family flag. When our youngest son received his MBA, he had a picture of himself with his graduation gown and flag. After restoring all our structures on our Family Farm, Belle Hampton, I had a photo taken of me and the flag in front of the house.

Another symbol you can use is to create a barn quilt. The American Barn Quilt has a history that dates back almost 300 years, when immigrants first arrived and used them as markers to help travelers find their way. These large, colorful, and decorative wooden panels or squares are typically mounted on the exterior of a barn or other agricultural building. During the Civil War, they were used for specific designs that guided the Underground Railroad. But in the 2000s, there was a surge in barn quilts in rural Ohio and Kentucky. The artists no longer stuck to the basic designs based on folklore. They became more elaborate. They often celebrate local history, honor family traditions, or beautify rural landscapes.

At our last family meeting, we designed our own barn quilt. We used some common symbols, like the North Star and Flock of Geese, to symbolize our direction as a family. We also added the three boar heads, which is a common theme in all of our symbols.

Although we were creating a barn quilt to represent our family, we also considered having an individual barn quilt to represent each unique person in the family. It is almost a rite of passage to display your quilt. Symbols such as flags, crests, and barn quilts are compelling representations of family heritage and lineage, which can be passed down through generations and encapsulate a family's values, history, and aspirations. These symbols unite generations, carrying the torch of familial pride and unity.

However, you are not obligated to use symbols from past generations. Use your creativity and encourage collaboration with the grandkids. The only rule is to think about what symbol represents your family. What makes your family distinctive? How do you want the uniqueness displayed?

This sense of pride and belonging, help our grandkids feel connected to their family's legacy and motivated to uphold its values through traditions.

Generations of Wisdom: The Intersection of Knowledge and Insight in Grandparenting

Knowledge and wisdom are two distinct but interconnected concepts, and they play essential roles in the lives of grandparents.

Knowledge refers to the information, facts, and skills acquired through learning, education, and experience. It involves understanding the "what" and "how" of various subjects or areas of expertise. For grandparents, knowledge may come from a variety of sources, including their own life experiences, formal education, and the wisdom passed down through generations. In today's digital age, they may also acquire knowledge through technology and the internet.

The concept of technology has undergone a profound transformation in today's world. Unlike previous generations, today's children were born into a digital landscape from a very young age, surrounded by a myriad of technological marvels that have become an integral part of their lives. From cell phones to game consoles and virtual pets like Webkinz, technology has shaped their experiences and perspectives in unique ways, ushering in a new era of digital natives.

Wisdom, on the other hand, goes beyond mere knowledge. It is the ability to apply knowledge, experience, and insight in a thoughtful and discerning manner to make sound judgments and decisions. Wisdom is about understanding the deeper implications of actions, considering the long-term consequences, and showing emotional intelligence. It often comes with age and life experience, but not every person automatically becomes wise. Like Father said in Mass if asked to draw a horse, draw a horse, and not everything around the horse like a cowboy with a lasso and the mountains in the background.

Your grade will count on following directions. Wisdom comes into play to know what to add and leave out. The advice from Father holds a valuable lesson in the importance of following directions and exercising wisdom in decision-making.

In the context of grandparents, here's how knowledge and wisdom play a role:

1.   Passing down knowledge: Grandparents can pass on their accumulated knowledge to younger generations. They may share life lessons, cultural traditions, family history, and practical skills that have been passed down through the years.

2.   Providing guidance: Wisdom allows grandparents to offer valuable guidance to their grandchildren. This can be in the form of advice on personal matters, relationships, career choices, or even navigating difficult situations.

3.   Emotional support: Wisdom enables grandparents to offer empathetic and compassionate support during challenging times.

They can draw from their experiences to provide comfort and understanding.

4.   Decision-making: When grandparents face important decisions, their wisdom can help them weigh options, consider consequences, and make informed choices.

5.   Interacting with technology: As technology continues to advance, grandparents can benefit from both knowledge and wisdom. Knowledge helps them stay up to date with the latest tools and gadgets, while wisdom helps them use technology responsibly and safely.

6.   Shaping family values: Grandparents often play a role in shaping family values and traditions. Their wisdom and experience contribute to the family's culture and identity.

It's important to note that while age can bring both knowledge and wisdom, not all older individuals automatically possess wisdom. Wisdom is cultivated through reflection, learning from mistakes, and an openness to growth and self-improvement. Some grandparents may have a wealth of knowledge but may still struggle with applying it wisely, while others may demonstrate profound wisdom despite having fewer formal qualifications.

In conclusion, knowledge and wisdom are valuable assets in the grandparents' space. Knowledge allows them to share information and expertise, while wisdom empowers them to provide guidance, and support, and make meaningful contributions to their families and communities. Do you plan to share wisdom or knowledge with the next generation?

Beyond Pages: Exploring the World of Reading

As we turn to reading, it's another way to reinforce the family's Legacy Capital. It fosters a sense of belonging, continuity, and shared purpose across generations.

These practices ensure that the wisdom and insights gained from past experiences are not lost but instead become a part of the family's ongoing narrative. By engaging with both historical texts and personal reflections, future generations can develop a deeper appreciation for their heritage and draw inspiration and guidance from the lessons embedded in these records.

For a passionate book lover like me, there's nothing quite like the magical world a book opens up. Each volume is a portal to a different time, place, or perspective, offering a chance to escape the mundane and embark on thrilling adventures, explore profound emotions, or delve deep into the realms of knowledge. In the realm of books, every page is an invitation to explore the infinite possibilities of the human imagination, making it a sanctuary for those who crave the magic of storytelling.

As authors, people often think that writing is our primary job. However, the most essential skill we possess is reading. We spend a lot of time and effort to ensure that every word we write ideally matches our thoughts and ideas. Additionally, we are avid readers of every genre, constantly seeking inspiration for topics, storylines, and phrasing.

My Journey Through the World of Book Reading Crafting a story takes skill, so I appreciate other authors' storytelling abilities. Even as a young child, I was enthralled with books. My sister bought me R. R. Tolkien's Lord of the Rings, which

I enthusiastically read cover to cover. Once I became a parent, we listened to the series on cassette tape with the kids as we drove. Two of my sons shared the passion and read it repeatedly for pleasure as adults.

However, my youngest son found the Lord of the Rings boring, with the mere thought of listening to it painful. So, as they say, two out of three ain't bad. But sharing books that are important to you and your family is vital to leaving a literary legacy.

My husband's grandfather wrote weekly "Thoughts on This and That." These writings were like a manual blog he shared with his friends and family through mail. Along with his reflections, he included chapters from his autobiography. Although I used to scan the autobiography chapters when they arrived, I eventually stored them in a file drawer in the attic, where they had been lost for many years.

After eleven moves, we emptied the attic, tossing some of the things that were collecting dust. I ran across the file, unaware of his autobiography, which I had read many years ago. Now that we have our children, I decided to share his fascinating story.

Choosing Books for Your Family Library

We have recently started a Family Library to promote a culture of reading, learning, and sharing among family members. Through literature, we aim to foster intellectual growth and bonding. Our library has a diverse collection of well-loved books covering various genres and not just limited to family history books.

Our library is broken down by subject matter. Jim Collins lists A must-read business book as 'From Good to Great.' We recommend '7 Habits of Highly Effective Families,' by Stephen Covey, for families and enterprises. For development, 'Creating Your Best Life,' by Caroline Miller. In the children's book category, 'The Marshmallow Mystery' by us, CJ Corki is a staple read, but there are others like 'Oh the Places You Will Go' by Dr. Suess.

However, each family library should be unique to your family. Sharing your most loved books growing up with children and grandchildren brings a special bond between family members. But where do you start?

To start building your family library, first identifying your goals is essential. Are you looking to create a collection of books suitable for young children, or are you hoping to include inspiring books for adult family members? Do you want to prioritize classic literature or focus on a particular theme, like family values? By considering these factors, you can better define the scope of your project and guide your book selections.

Choose a location for the books. Do you want them to be physical books you can have when everyone visits? Or would you prefer digital books? Alternatively, would you like to share a list of book recommendations? Your decision should depend on everyone's physical location.

Think about whether they are spread out around the world or are local to you. Also, consider your budget. Are the books costly? If money is not an issue, would you like to purchase books for everyone in the family?

Promoting Reading as a Family Activity

Make reading a family activity by encouraging regular reading. Set aside dedicated reading times when everyone can read together, discuss books, or take turns reading aloud. If you have distant young grandchildren, consider recording a reading out loud or using a virtual call to read to them. Start a family reading group to discuss the books.

Promote reading challenges to encourage reading and celebrate achievements but be mindful of individual abilities and preferences. Two of our sons have dyslexia, which slows their rate of reading. Offer alternative options like audiobooks to ensure everyone can participate. Remember, the primary focus should be on promoting reading for enjoyment rather than creating pressure to meet unrealistic goals.

Continue to grow your family library by adding new books and materials over time. You can consider family trips to bookstores, library visits, or online purchases to keep the collection fresh and engaging. Solicit family member recommendations or visit favorite author websites since they often give book recommendations. However, what you add should match the purpose of your family library.

Leaving a literary legacy is the greatest gift you can give as a grandparent. The gift of knowledge, enjoyment, and family history will be something they will remember for a lifetime.

Food Superstitions: Stirring up the Quirky Beliefs Around Eating

Have you ever caught yourself knocking on wood or staying away from crossing paths with black cats? Don't worry, I do the same!

Family food superstitions, passed down through generations, serve as a unique form of Legacy Capital, preserving cultural heritage and reinforcing familial bonds through shared traditions and beliefs.

Across the world, age-old traditions, customs, and beliefs have been passed down through generations in every culture and society. These practices are deeply rooted in our collective history and serve as a shield against misfortune and ill fate. One common thread among these rituals is the consumption of specific foods believed to safeguard against bad luck.

Welcome to the intriguing world of superstitions, foods, and actions that people take to steer clear of misfortune. Now, doesn't that sound heady? But let's step back for a moment and explore the captivating customs in our family's past and find a way to preserve them for future generations. Food, glorious food. Is it worth waiting for? Yes, it's an excerpt from the renowned musical

Oliver!, but it illustrates food's profound significance, brimming with beliefs and customs. Across different cultures, each of us consumes specific foods to ward off misfortune, banish evil, and welcome good luck. Let's investigate the fascinating world of meals consumed to avoid ill omens and safeguard oneself from misfortune. One or two of them may already be a part of your life.

China, known for its rich culture and vast food diversity, has maintained a longstanding tradition around food and luck. When my husband and I honeymooned in China, we enjoyed the customary tradition of indulging in longevity noodles on his birthday. It represented a long life, but the key was that they were always left uncut, and you would need to slurp the noodles or tie them around your chopsticks to ensure the "bad energy" didn't escape.

New Year's Eve and New Year's Day are ripe with superstitions, and actions taken to ensure the future is bright. I have a friend who faithfully consumes twelve grapes at the stroke of midnight on New Year's Eve. Each grape symbolizes good fortune for one month of the upcoming year. This tradition was brought to the United States by his grandparents, who immigrated from Europe.

Let's get local. For over four decades, my sisters have lived in the Southern US, and during that time, a new tradition has become a part of our family: enjoying black-eyed peas and collard greens on New Year's Day. According to this tradition, black-eyed peas symbolize luck, while collard greens represent money, ensuring a financially booming year ahead.

I embraced this "new" family tradition, and we eagerly prepared these dishes by washing, dicing, and cooking them according to the recipe. However, when we finally tasted them, it was like chewing on waxy paper and bitter greens. We wondered if this unpleasant experience was a necessary sacrifice for the promised good fortune. Despite our urge to gag, we reluctantly ate the unappetizing meal. Only after sharing our ordeal with our brother-in-law did we discover the secret to improving these dishes: spices and bacon. It became clear that consulting a native about cultural expectations is often essential, or maybe he should have made the first batch.

In my Polish American family, the ultimate expression of love during Christmas is sharing an oplatek. This thin, flat, and seemingly flavorless wafer holds a significant meaning. And we are not the only ones. Before indulging in the Christmas Eve feast, numerous families with Eastern European heritage, including those from Poland, join in this age-old tradition that spans generations.

At the start of dinner, my dad would take the flavorless Christmas wafer and express his hopes for our mom in the upcoming year. Then, mom would break off a piece of the oplatek and eat it. She then reciprocated the good wishes and shared the wafer back with him. But the tradition doesn't end there. The ceremonial sharing of wafers and extending good wishes continues with older relatives, guests, and children, starting with the oldest.

Customs and traditions seem never-ending, offering a multitude of captivating stories. These culinary rituals provide me with a sense of comfort, a connection to the past, and a feeling of empowerment over my life's path. Reflecting upon the reasons behind these practices, I can't help but contemplate the countless generations before me who have taken the very same actions. At that moment, we are united and bound by shared experiences throughout the years.

Does this make you think about your cultural customs? Well, that's good. They offer various traditions that add excitement to our daily lives and great stories to tell. We all have a history filled with stories of survival, resilience, and a strong belief in the influence of food on our destiny...pass it on!

By embracing and sharing these beliefs, we ensure that future generations develop a deeper understanding and respect for the diverse traditions within our families. Let's help the kids understand our family's traditions and customs and remind them of the significance of cultural traditions.

Let's pause momentarily to admire the culinary customs that may be part of your family's heritage. Not only are they enjoyable and excellent conversation starters, but they are also crucial in the efforts to uphold and pass down these valuable traditions. Our responsibility is to ensure they are treasured and carried forward to future generations.

Now let's turn our attention to another timeless tradition: the simple yet profound act of crafting handwritten notes to impart wisdom and love to our beloved grandkids.

Preserving Family History: The Power of a Handwritten Letter

I had an epiphany last night and had to share! Handwritten letters are like warm hugs on paper, carrying the personal touch that emails can never quite capture. What do you think?

By sharing these written accounts, families can maintain a continuous dialogue across generations, ensuring that the knowledge and traditions that shape the family's identity and values are preserved and passed down, strengthening the family's legacy.

Hear me out. You and I live in the same fast-paced digital world. I have always been a communicator, but my communication, which used to be slower paced, has morphed into mostly texting and social media posts. In this modern era of smartphones, laptops, and iPads, letter writing may seem obsolete. As quick, short emails, tweets, and text messages have replaced heartfelt, handwritten messages, children are becoming less familiar with this traditional form of communication. However, we must keep this important tradition.

I have to ask you...When was the last time you wrote and sent a handwritten letter?

It may seem like a relic of the past. However, we have a special gift. That gift is to help our grandkids and, yes, even our kids discover the power of this timeless form of communication. Remember that feeling when you received a letter in the mail? Handwritten letters are not only nostalgic and meaningful, but they also can hold immense value in a child's life. It doesn't matter if you live minutes away, halfway around the world, or somewhere in between; the power and impact of receiving a handwritten letter cannot be underestimated. Through these letters, we can share stories and experiences, ask questions, and, yes, even provide advice, creating a lasting bond and imparting wisdom in a personal and memorable way.

Let's look beyond the immediate impact. Those handwritten letters also extend to the preservation of family history and traditions. These letters serve as historical artifacts, documenting personal anecdotes, joys, and challenges of our lives. They become cherished heirlooms that can be passed down through generations, providing a glimpse into the past and keeping memories alive.

Regrettably, I do not have any handwritten letters, except for one sent to me in the past. A priceless letter was written by my mom, who shared her thoughts about the person I have become, the decisions I have made, and what she wishes for me in the future. I have referred to this letter so often that it is now well-worn with love and tears. Sometimes, I bring it out to feel her close by now that she is no longer with us; other times, I re-read the things she was most proud of about me. Her legacy and mine will be passed on to future generations.

So, how do you begin? Remember what it was like holding that pen in your hand, writing well-turned letters on the page as you conveyed warmth, care, and thoughtfulness? That is your starting point. Next, share something you are passionate about and then ask for a response on their thoughts. This tangible expression of emotions creates a deeper connection between the sender and recipient, fostering a sense of intimacy and closeness that electronic communication struggles to achieve.

The added benefit of receiving a handwritten letter is that it offers a refreshing break from this technological overload. It forces children to slow down, savor the anticipation, and engage in a more deliberate and meaningful exchange.

In addition to the emotional benefits, sending and receiving handwritten letters can positively impact a child's cognitive development. We talk about learning differences that children may have, and reading and deciphering someone's handwriting might be an additional obstacle, but it can also help identify learning issues earlier. Even if this is challenging, it can help improve literacy skills as children learn to recognize letters, words, and sentence structure. An added value of language comprehension, word formation, grammar, punctuation, and creativity to form meaningful sentences.

Also, the handwritten letter doesn't have to be a one-way street. Your grandchild can also write back to you. Composing a letter will encourage creativity, critical thinking, and problem-solving as children effectively navigate how to convey their thoughts and emotions on paper. When children write letters, they take ownership of their thoughts and ideas. They realize that their words matter and can elicit reactions, prompting them to be careful with what they write.

Depending on their age, children can also express themselves and develop their storytelling skills by creating beautiful cards or letters with colorful pens, pencils, stickers, or other crafting materials.

I hope I have shared the significance of writing handwritten letters to preserve handwritten letters as legacies, exploring the emotional connection they forge, the intimacy they offer, and the enduring impact they can have on the recipients and their descendants. Whether it's a heartfelt note of advice or wisdom, we can create lasting memories, strengthen family ties, and nourish our children's emotional and cognitive development in a way that no digital communication can match.

Writing letters to your family is considered Legacy Capital because it preserves personal thoughts, emotions, and experiences that can be cherished and learned from by future generations.

So, let's embrace the art of letter-writing and ensure that our grandkids experience the joy and benefits it brings.

My Treasures, Your Trash: Uncovering the Stories Behind Grandma's Past

From the heartfelt sentiments in handwritten letters to the personal treasures that hold immense value to us but might appear as mere trash to others, our lives are filled with artifacts that carry profound meaning and significance, contributing to our Legacy Capital.

I am guessing that you are no different from me. You've got "stuff." Yes, we all have "stuff." Our stuff collection probably began 40+ years ago when we innocently compiled a list of gift ideas for our wedding registry. A Lenox place setting for one, until you reach serving for 12...people, and you did. Christmas, birthday, and anniversary ideas? Add another Waterford glass or, like my mom, a yearly Hummel figurine given lovingly to her from her daughters until she had at least 18 of them!

So, let's play it forward. We may be downsizing, or someone got the short straw for cleaning Grandma's attic or basement. Here is often where a treasure trove of forgotten items lives. Among these items lie stories waiting to be discovered.

The seemingly mundane trash accumulated over the years can hold secrets and memories that provide a glimpse into our past.

One of my many "special" trash items was a baby grand piano that I recently sent to piano heaven. Even though pianos are not a typical purchase for the minimalist generation, I had to share the story of why it was purchased, and pulled out pictures of us playing, dancing, and singing around it over the last 37 years. My daughter was shocked to hear the backstory, and the pictures were a delightful journey of nostalgia, history, and personal anecdotes. It was a priceless offering to the insight into my life. Let's take advantage of that opportunity to share those stories.

Another one of the most intriguing aspects of letting others explore our treasures together is the opportunity to learn about our lifestyle. Whether it is old cooking utensils, vintage clothing, or outdated electronics, each discarded item communicates a story about how we lived and what was important to each of us. Perhaps someone will stumble upon a collection of worn-out, stained, and well-used recipe cards, hinting at culinary adventures and cherished family recipes. Okay, that recipe reference is not me and is not something you will find in my collection, but if you look further, you will find my mom's and her mom's recipes with, unfortunately, many untold stories. Don't let that be you!

Exploring our trash can also reveal the context of our time. Decade-old newspapers, magazines, and advertisements can offer invaluable insights into the news, fashion, and trends of bygone eras. Remember, digital media was not the norm while we were growing up.

Together, with our kids and grandkids we can analyze these items to understand better the historical events that influenced our generation. Those old newspapers, hidden away, might provide in-depth coverage of a pivotal moment in history. Remember where you were when JFK was killed? The front-page article on when we first landed on the moon or even an old Cosmopolitan, the magazine, not the drink. All of these can present a snapshot of the latest trends and influences of the time. By diving into our trash, they can connect with our personal history and the broader historical narrative. And many of them may have never had the pleasure of touching newsprint and getting it all over their fingers!

So, I am encouraging you, no, imploring you, to explore your trash, aka treasures, with your family now since that is where our personal stories and memories lie. I am betting that if we wait until after we are gone, some, many, or maybe all our treasures may seem insignificant at first glance and could and will quickly become junk and placed in the recycle bin.

The time is now! Bring the grandkids over, make a day of it, and take a scavenger hunt through time. For us, this can trigger memories and stories that will never be passed down through generations if we don't share them now. You might come across an old photo album filled with pictures capturing long-forgotten family vacations, weddings, and celebrations, sparking conversations and narratives about loved ones who are no longer with us. Tell the story...now!

Remember, the sentimental value of trash in our attic or basement cannot be overlooked. These items witnessed the passage of time, the growth of a family, and the trials and triumphs of life. They are priceless and something we must share with those we love. These are part of our legacy and hold immeasurable sentimental worth beyond their physical appearance, but only if we pass on the meaning.

Together, as we examine these items, we become time travelers, unraveling the threads that connect our multiple family generations.

So, the next time you find yourself faced with the task of clearing out the attic or basement, take a moment to appreciate the untold stories lurking among the treasures and be sure to share them with the kids!

Legacy Capital Conclusion

As you can see, Legacy Capital is not just a concept—it is a powerful force that connects all generations. We can shape a shared identity and purpose that resonates through time. It will have a lasting impact on those fortunate enough to inherit it.

This bridge between past, present, and future is a treasure trove of wisdom, traditions, and stories that shape how we see ourselves and the world around us. Ultimately, Legacy Capital is a gift that keeps on giving, empowering future generations to carry forward the legacy of their ancestors with pride, resilience, and a deep sense of connection.

So, establish those strong connections that will open opportunities for meaningful conversations, genuine empathy, and a sense of belonging with our grandkids.

Legacy Capital
Bingo

This bingo celebrates the cherished traditions and stories passed down through our family from one generation to the next. It's more than just relics; it's about the memories and affection they represent. The ultimate reward is the thrill of exploring our heritage in a fun and engaging manner.

What is your favorite family tradition?	Make a family tradition food	Research where your family comes from	Find the names of your great-great grandmothers	FInd a picture of grandpa/grandma when they were your age
Find out the story behind your name	Make a family tree	Record a story you want the next generation to remember	Start a time capsule of your life	Create a coat of arms
Ask your parents for a funny story from their youth	Visit a place that is significant to the family	CJ CORKI	Write a letter to future you	Look up one military record from your family
Find a family heirloom	How would you like to be remembered?	What traditions do you want to continue?	Plan a family reunion	Try an activity that your ancestors did
Make a family flag	Share a story you heard about someone in your past	Start a new tradition	Go to a 4th of July parade	Visit a American history museum

LEGACY CAPITAL ACTIVITY

Goals

How can you foster a deeper understanding of your roots, inspire pride in your family's history, and encourage your grandchildren to cherish and build upon the legacy they will inherit?

Books:

- Families Around the World by Margriet Ruurs and Jessica Rae Gordon

- Story Swapping: A Children's Picture about a Beloved Family Tradition by Vassi Rombis

- A Crocodile in the Family by Kitty Black

- Name Your Favorite: _____

Questions to Ask:

- If you could save something special for your family, what would it be?

- What is your favorite family story?

- What is something fun you do with your cousins or siblings?

Conclusion

As you reflect on your past performances and transition from being the star performer, consider the different forms of capital we discussed in the circus ring: Financial, Intellectual, Human, Social, Spiritual, and Legacy. Think about the valuable insights you've gained that you can share with the rising generation. First, consider utilizing Financial Capital to develop other forms of capital, not just increasing the money itself. Second, use Intellectual Capital to feed ongoing improvement and a thirst for knowledge. Third, Human Capital can create a vibrant and joyful environment when nurtured effectively. Social Capital, when cultivated, can lead to strong family bonds. Spiritual Capital is cultivated through core values and beliefs, akin to an acrobat entrusting their faith in their circus family. Lastly, legacy Capital represents your role as a unifier rather than the central figure of the family. Balancing and nurturing each type of capital will not only enrich your own life but also positively impact future generations. So step into the spotlight, join us today, and let's create a show that leaves everyone in awe!

About the Author

Renowned for their knack for crafting vivid and relatable tales, CJ Corki continues to captivate readers with Not My Money: Overcoming the Elephant in the Room, the third book in a beloved series dedicated to grandparents. Through their masterful storytelling, CJ Corki invites readers into a world where love, wisdom, and laughter are as valuable as any treasure.

CJ Corki cherishes the opportunity to enrich lives and spark imaginations, much like their father once did. Embracing the timeless power of the written word, they continue a cherished family tradition, transporting readers to extraordinary worlds where the bonds of family are the true wealth. By holding the baton of storytelling firmly in hand, CJ Corki underscores the priceless nature of family connections and the lasting value of shared stories.

Visit us at
cjcorki.com
or
Contact us at
author@cjcorki.com

www.ingramcontent.com/pod-product-compliance
Lightning Source LLC
Chambersburg PA
CBHW060250150626
46553CB00019BA/1579